INGMAR BERGMAN

AN ARTIST'S JOURNEY

ON STAGE · ON SCREEN · IN PRINT

Edited by Roger W. Oliver

ARCADE PUBLISHING · NEW YORK

FIRST EDITION

Library of Congress Cataloging-in-Publication Data

Ingmar Bergman : an artist's journey — on stage, on screen, in print / edited by Roger W. Oliver.
— 1st ed.
p.   cm.
ISBN 1-55970-295-8
1. Bergman, Ingmar, 1918–   — Criticism and interpretation.
I. Bergman, Ingmar, 1918–   .   II. Oliver, Roger W., 1945–   .
PN1998.3.B47I54   1995
791.43'0233'092 — dc20   94-46211

Published in the United States by Arcade Publishing, Inc., New York

Distributed by Little, Brown and Company

10 9 8 7 6 5 4 3 2 1

HP

Designed by Jeffrey L. Ward

PRINTED IN THE UNITED STATES OF AMERICA

"Each Film Is My Last," by Ingmar Bergman, copyright ©1966 by and reprinted by permission of the *Drama Review*, Vol. 11, No. 1, T-33, Fall 1966; "Remembering Alf Sjöberg" from *The Magic Lantern*, by Ingmar Bergman, translated by Joan Tate, translation copyright ©1988 by Joan Tate, original copyright ©1987 by Ingmar Bergman, reprinted by permission of Viking Penguin, a division of Penguin Books USA Inc.; "Bergman's Best Intentions," copyright ©1991 by Lasse Bergström, translation copyright ©1992 by and reprinted by permission of Richard Nord, originally published in *Scanorama*, May 1992; "Through a Life Darkly," ©1988 by Woody Allen, reprinted by permission of Rollins and Joffe for the author, originally published in the *New York Times Book Review*, September 18, 1988; "On Ingmar Bergman" from *The Films in My Life*, by François Truffaut, copyright ©1975 by Flammarion, translation copyright ©1978 by Simon & Schuster, Inc., reprinted by permission of Simon & Schuster; "Bergmanorama," by Jean-Luc Godard, copyright ©1988 by and reprinted by permission of the Swedish Film Institute, originally published in *Ingmar Bergman at 70: A Tribute*, special issue of *Chaplin Film Magazine*, edited by Lars Åhlander, 1988; "Working with Bergman: Excerpts from a Seminar with Liv Ullmann," copyright ©1973 by and reprinted by permission of Liv Ullmann, originally published in *American Film*, March 1973; "The Bergman Vaccination Method," by Erland Josephson, copyright ©1988 by and reprinted by permission of the Swedish Film Institute, originally published in *Ingmar Bergman at 70: A Tribute*, special issue of *Chaplin Film Magazine*, edited by Lars Åhlander, 1988; "A Letter to Ingmar Bergman," by Max von Sydow, copyright ©1988 by and reprinted by permission of the Swedish Film Institute, originally published in *Ingmar Bergman at 70: A Tribute*, special issue of *Chaplin Film Magazine*, edited by Lars Åhlander, 1988; "Confessions of a Bergman Co-Worker," by Gunnel Lindblom, copyright ©1988 by and reprinted by permission of the Swedish Film Institute, originally published in *Ingmar Bergman at 70: A Tribute*, special issue of *Chaplin Film Magazine*, edited by Lars Åhlander, 1988; "Some Thoughts about an Old Colleague on His Way to Canonization," by Eva Dahlbeck, copyright ©1988 by and reprinted by permission of the Swedish Film Institute, originally published in *Ingmar Bergman at 70: A Tribute*, special issue of *Chaplin Film Magazine*, edited by Lars Åhlander, 1988; "Bergman on Stage and Screen: Excerpts from a Seminar with Bibi Andersson," copyright ©1977 by and reprinted by permission of Bibi Andersson, originally published in *American Film*, March 1977; "The Northern Protestant," copyright ©1960 by James Baldwin, reprinted by permission of the James Baldwin Estate, originally published in *Esquire* and collected in *Nobody Knows My Name: More Notes of a Native Son*, published by Vintage Books; "A Filmmaker in the Borderland: Bergman and Cultural Traditions," by Mikael Timm, copyright ©1988 by and reprinted by permission of the Swedish Film Institute, originally published in *Ingmar Bergman at 70: A Tribute*, special issue of *Chaplin Film Magazine*, edited by Lars Åhlander, 1988; "The Significance of Ingmar Bergman," by Jörn Donner, copyright ©1988 by and reprinted by permission of the Swedish Film Institute, originally published in *Ingmar Bergman at 70: A Tribute*, special issue of *Chaplin Film Magazine*, edited by Lars Åhlander, 1988; "Bergman's Trilogy: Tradition and Innovation," by Roger W. Oliver, copyright ©1992 by and reprinted by permission of The Johns Hopkins University Press, originally published in *Performing Arts Journal #40*, Vol. 14, No. 1, January 1992; "Bergman as Novelist," by Caryn James, copyright ©1994 by and reprinted by permission of the *New York Times*, originally published as "Ingmar Bergman Adds to the Mosaic of Autobiography" in the *New York Times*, April 22, 1994; "The Imagined Past in Ingmar Bergman's *The Best Intentions*," copyright ©1994 by Rochelle Wright; "The Typically Swedish in Ingmar Bergman," by Maaret Koskinen, copyright ©1988 by and reprinted by permission of the Swedish Film Institute, originally published in *Chaplin Film Magazine*, 25th anniversary issue, edited by Lars Åhlander, 1984; " 'Manhattan Surrounded by Ingmar Bergman,' " copyright ©1994 by Birgitta Steene; "Winter Songs," copyright ©1994 by John H. Lahr, reprinted by permission of Georges Borchardt, Inc. for the author, originally published in *The New Yorker*, October 3, 1994.

Photo credits appear on page 161.

INGMAR BERGMAN

AN ARTIST'S JOURNEY
ON STAGE · ON SCREEN · IN PRINT

CONTENTS

LIST OF ILLUSTRATIONS   vii

INTRODUCTION *Roger W. Oliver*   ix

PART ONE: BERGMAN ON BERGMAN

EACH FILM IS MY LAST *Ingmar Bergman*   3

REMEMBERING ALF SJÖBERG *Ingmar Bergman*   13

BERGMAN'S BEST INTENTIONS *Lasse Bergström*   16

PART TWO: DIRECTORS ON BERGMAN

THROUGH A LIFE DARKLY *Woody Allen*   25

ON INGMAR BERGMAN *François Truffaut*   31

BERGMANORAMA *Jean-Luc Godard*   37

PART THREE: ACTORS ON BERGMAN

WORKING WITH BERGMAN: EXCERPTS FROM A SEMINAR WITH *LIV ULLMANN*   45

THE BERGMAN VACCINATION METHOD *Erland Josephson*   53

A LETTER TO INGMAR BERGMAN *Max von Sydow*   57

CONFESSIONS OF A BERGMAN CO-WORKER *Gunnel Lindblom*   59

SOME THOUGHTS ABOUT AN OLD COLLEAGUE ON HIS WAY TO CANONIZATION *Eva Dahlbeck*   64

BERGMAN ON STAGE AND SCREEN: EXCERPTS FROM A SEMINAR WITH *BIBI ANDERSSON*   69

PART FOUR: REFLECTIONS ON BERGMAN

THE NORTHERN PROTESTANT *James Baldwin*   79

A FILMMAKER IN THE BORDERLAND: BERGMAN AND CULTURAL TRADITIONS *Mikael Timm*   88

CONTENTS

THE SIGNIFICANCE OF INGMAR BERGMAN *Jörn Donner*   99

BERGMAN'S TRILOGY: TRADITION AND INNOVATION *Roger W. Oliver*   105

BERGMAN AS NOVELIST *Caryn James*   112

THE IMAGINED PAST IN INGMAR BERGMAN'S *THE BEST INTENTIONS* *Rochelle Wright*   116

THE TYPICALLY SWEDISH IN INGMAR BERGMAN *Maaret Koskinen*   126

"MANHATTAN SURROUNDED BY INGMAR BERGMAN": THE AMERICAN RECEPTION
OF A SWEDISH FILMMAKER *Birgitta Steene*   137

WINTER SONGS *John Lahr*   155

ACKNOWLEDGMENTS   161

Illustrations

Ingmar Bergman directing Strindberg's *A Dream Play*	x
The young Ingmar Bergman on location	4
Bergman directing *Crisis,* with cinematographer Gösta Roosling	6
Bergman with Signe Hasso and Alf Kjellin during the filming of *This Can't Happen Here*	9
Alf Sjöberg directing a scene from Bergman's screenplay *Torment*	15
Börje Ahlstedt and Solveig Ternström in Ibsen's *Peer Gynt*	17
Börje Ahlstedt as Peer Gynt	19
Jarl Kulle and cast members of *King Lear*	21
A scene from *Illicit Interlude* with Maj-Britt Nilsson and Annalisa Ericson	26
Stockholm's outer archipelago as filmed in *Illicit Interlude*, with Maj-Britt Nilsson	28–29
Lars Ekborg and Harriet Andersson in *Monika*	33
Harriet Andersson as Monika in *Monika*	35
Anders Ek as the white circus clown and Gudrun Brost in *The Naked Night*	38
Harriet Andersson in *Monika*	40
Liv Ullmann and Max von Sydow in *Shame*	47
Bergman directing Liv Ullmann on the set of *Autumn Sonata*	50
Bengt Ekerot as Death and Max von Sydow as the Knight in *The Seventh Seal*	55
Max von Sydow with Bibi Andersson in *The Seventh Seal*	58
Bergman on the set of *The Seventh Seal* with Bengt Ekerot	60
The Dance of Death in *The Seventh Seal*	63
Eva Dahlbeck as Désirée Armfeldt in *Smiles of a Summer Night*	65
Victor Sjöström remembering the past in *Wild Strawberries*	67
Bibi Andersson, Liv Ullmann, Sven Nykvist, and Ingmar Bergman during the filming of *Persona*	70
Bergman in conference with cinematographer Sven Nykvist	71

ILLUSTRATIONS

Split image of Bibi Andersson and Liv Ullmann in *Persona* — 72–73

Bibi Andersson and Liv Ullmann in *Persona* — 75

A scene from *Through a Glass Darkly* — 81

Ingmar Bergman with Gunnar Björnstrand during the filming of *Winter Light* — 82–83

Gunnel Lindblom with Jörgen Lindström and Ingrid Thulin in *The Silence* — 85

A scene from Strindberg's *A Dream Play* — 89

A scene from Strindberg's *A Dream Play* — 90

Lena Olin and Per Myrberg in Strindberg's *A Dream Play* — 92

Peter Stormare and Lena Olin in Strindberg's *Miss Julie* — 95

Max von Sydow with Bergman during the filming of *Hour of the Wolf* — 100

Bergman, Ulf Johanson, and Liv Ullmann during the filming of *Face to Face* — 102

Bibi Andersson and Thommy Berggren in Eugene O'Neill's *Long Day's Journey into Night* — 107

Pernilla August and Per Mattsson in Ibsen's *A Doll's House* — 108

Pernilla August in *A Doll's House* — 110

Bergman and Erland Josephson on the set of *Fanny and Alexander* — 113

Bergman with Bertil Guve during the filming of *Fanny and Alexander* — 115

Bergman with the children in the cast of *Fanny and Alexander* — 117

Bergman orchestrating the dinner party of *Fanny and Alexander* — 119

Gunnar Björnstrand as Filip Landahl in *Fanny and Alexander* — 122

Bergman with longtime cinematographer Sven Nykvist — 123

A scene from *Cries and Whispers* — 127

Bergman with Ingrid Thulin in *Cries and Whispers* — 130

Bergman blocking Liv Ullmann in *Cries and Whispers* — 133

Max von Sydow and cast members of Ibsen's *The Wild Duck* — 138

Bibi Andersson and Lille Terselius in Shakespeare's *Twelfth Night* — 140

A scene from *Hamlet* — 143

Peter Stormare and Per Myrberg in the ghost scene of *Hamlet* — 147

The final scene of *Hamlet* — 151

Anita Björk and Stina Ekblad in Yukio Mishima's *Madame de Sade* — 152

Bergman with Stina Ekblad and Marie Richardsson on the set of *Madame de Sade* — 156

Bibi Andersson in Shakespeare's *A Winter's Tale* — 157

Bergman with the set model of *A Winter's Tale* — 159

INTRODUCTION

When Ingmar Bergman announced in 1983 that *Fanny and Alexander* would be his final film, many people greeted the news of his intended retirement with skepticism. After all, he was at the height of his cinematic powers with this rich, multilayered work. Although Bergman had written and directed films for almost forty years, *Fanny and Alexander* seemed to break new ground both in its exploration of his own psyche and personal experience and in the creation of images of great archetypal power. Even though Bergman cited the physical demands of filmmaking as his reason for stopping, many of his admirers believed (and of course hoped) that he would not be able to stay away.

In the dozen years since *Fanny and Alexander,* however, it has become evident that Bergman's "retirement" was only from one particular segment of his artistic life. And, unlike those artists who seek challenges in new fields after having made their mark in the one they are best known for, Bergman was merely continuing two lifelong interests, the theater and writing. Both had been central to his identity as an artist from the begin-

ning of his career. In addition, having brought his filmmaking skills to television in 1957, he actively continues to work in that medium as writer and director. If Bergman the film director was the persona best known to his international public, Bergman the writer (primarily of his own film and television scripts) and Bergman the stage director were never slighted in favor of his more "famous" self.

It is, in fact, Bergman's ability to sustain careers in theater, film, and television, all at the highest levels of artistic excellence and achievement, that makes him a unique figure as a creative and interpretive artist. While there have been (and continue to be) many great directors whose careers have encompassed both theater and the camera media, in every other case it is possible to state with near certainty that their major impact has been in one area or the other. From the start of his artistic life in the 1940s to his retirement from the cinema in the 1980s, not only did Bergman alternate between stage and screen (both large and small) but he was generally acknowledged to be a consummate master

Ingmar Bergman on the first day of rehearsal for A Dream Play *at the Royal Dramatic Theater of Sweden in 1986*

in each realm. Although he has directed few opera productions, even there he has made his presence felt, with versions of *The Rake's Progress* for the Royal Swedish Opera, *The Merry Widow* for the Malmö Municipal Theater, and *The Magic Flute* for film, all of which are considered landmarks. In recent years he has made an important mark as a writer. Both fiction (*The Best Intentions* and *Sunday's Children*) and nonfiction (*The Magic Lantern* and *Images*) further solidify his identity as a twentieth-century artistic Renaissance man.

Although the origin and nature of genius are impossible to pinpoint, in Bergman's case there are certain cultural precedents and institutions that can help us better understand why he refused to restrict himself to one particular genre or medium. As a twentieth-century Swedish writer and director, he would, perhaps inevitably, have been influenced by August Strindberg, who died only six years before Bergman was born. One of the founders of theatrical modernism, Strindberg was not only novelist and playwright, but also painter, photographer, and alchemist. Among Bergman's earliest artistic endeavors were stagings of Strindberg plays, first in his childhood marionette theater and later in a youth theater he directed before embarking on his professional career. Bergman has returned to Strindberg again and again throughout his theatrical life, directing *Miss Julie, The Ghost Sonata,* and *A Dream Play* in several different versions, in some cases for radio and television as well as theater.

It is easiest to see Strindberg's influence on Bergman in their depictions of the painful relationships between men and women, especially within the institution of marriage. Such Strindberg masterworks as *The Father* and *Dance of Death* can be said to anticipate Bergman's exploration of similar themes in the film *The Passion of Anna* and in the six-episode television version of *Scenes from a Marriage* that was later condensed into a film for theatrical release. Yet it is not just in subject matter but also in the nature of Strindberg's career, characterized by restless experimentation both within and between the forms of expression he explored, that Bergman could have found a multidisciplinary model toward which to aspire.

The fact that one of those disciplines was film should not be surprising given the era in which Bergman grew to maturity. Cinema was not just a phenomenon growing in international popularity during the 1920s and 1930s; it was one emphatically embraced in Sweden. In the twenties Svensk Filmindustri, later the production company for many of Bergman's films, became the main source of films in Scandinavia. Major silent film directors, including Georg af Klecker (whom Bergman writes about in his play *The Last Scream*), Mauritz Stiller, and Viktor Sjöström (who played the old man in Bergman's *Wild Strawberries*), were making international reputations with their films. According to film historian Robert Sklar, in *Film: An International History of the Medium,* "No countries with populations so small, British film historian Forsyth Hardy wrote in the early 1950s, had made so great a contribution to world cinema as Sweden and Denmark (and this was before Sweden's Ingmar Bergman became famous as a leading director of international art cinema)."

This contribution would have included not only the films of the directors named above, but also those of Alf Sjöberg, who had a great influence on Bergman's artistic life. Sjöberg's career as a filmmaker embraced both silent and sound eras. When his film of Strindberg's *Miss Julie* won the Palm d'Or at the Cannes Film Festival in 1950, it was the first Swedish film to be so honored. Sjöberg served as more than a model and inspiration for Bergman. In 1944 he directed *Torment*, Bergman's first screenplay to be realized on celluloid, the success of which facilitated Bergman's film directorial debut the following year. Sjöberg, whose film career was soon to be eclipsed by his younger colleague's, directed another of Bergman's scripts, *Last Couple Out*, in 1956.

Sjöberg's place in Swedish cinema and Sjöberg's importance for Bergman, however, extend far beyond their two collaborations. Despite his success as a filmmaker, Sjöberg's major achievement was as a theater director. For almost half a century his productions at the Royal Dramatic Theater (the Dramaten) in Stockholm were singled out for their interpretive power and theatrical imagination. When asked why he had directed almost no plays by Shakespeare at the Dramaten during the years when he and Sjöberg were in residence there, Bergman replied that there was no reason to do so, since Sjöberg's productions were so good. In an act of homage to his fellow director, after Sjöberg's death Bergman filmed for television Sjöberg's final stage production, Molière's *The School for Wives,* completing the circle begun with *Torment.*

If Sjöberg thus served as a precedent for a director who could combine important careers in theater and film, he also symbolized continuity in his stage career. As an actor, Sjöberg appeared at the Dramaten in over fifty productions from 1923 to 1931, and from 1930 to 1980 he directed 138 productions. The Dramaten, where as a boy Bergman first experienced a live theatrical performance — directed by Sjöberg — has been Bergman's theatrical home since 1961. He continues to direct one or two productions a year there, combining reinterpretations of the classics with stagings of contemporary plays from the international repertory.

The Dramaten not only allows Bergman to work with many of Sweden's most distinguished actors, but also provides him the opportunity to continue associations that extend back to his early career. Erland Josephson, who played the title role in Bergman's 1994 production of George Tabori's *The Goldberg Variations,* has known the director since 1939. He appeared in many of Bergman's films, including *The Magician, Scenes from a Marriage,* and *Fanny and Alexander,* and was once Bergman's, and Sjöberg's, boss, when he ran the Dramaten, a position Bergman also held at one time. Bibi Andersson, whose recent stage collaborations with Bergman include *Long Day's Journey into Night, The Goldberg Variations,* and

The Winter's Tale, has worked with Bergman since the 1950s. Although Max von Sydow's recent performances at the Dramaten have not been in Bergman productions, there are plans for Bergman to write and direct a play for and with von Sydow.

Bergman's long association with von Sydow illustrates how the director's career always alternated between stage and screen. (In 1950 Bergman compared the theater to a loyal wife, and film to a costly and demanding mistress, but twenty years later he revised his assessment and said, "Now I'm living in bigamy.") During the fifties, for example, in the summer Bergman directed von Sydow in the films *The Seventh Seal, The Magician,* and *The Virgin Spring;* during the theater season the actor played at the Malmö Municipal Theater as Faust, Peer Gynt, Alceste in Molière's *The Misanthrope,* and Brick in *Cat on a Hot Tin Roof,* all directed by Bergman. Von Sydow himself sees a strong connection between Bergman's film and theater work, which a comparison of photographs from *Faust* and *The Seventh Seal,* for example, seems to document.

There is no doubt that Bergman's work in the various media has affected his artistic vision as a whole. Theatrical performance has often had an important role in his films, from *The Naked Night* to *Fanny and Alexander,* and a cinematic approach to space and time can be seen in such theater productions as *A Doll's House* and *Madame de Sade.* It is doubtful that Bergman's richly textured production of *The Winter's Tale* would have been possible if he had not created *Fanny and Alexander* first. When he directs a play, he shapes the text as a writer would, cutting and rearranging material, sometimes in a radical way. Although the plays he chooses to direct do not have the same biographical and personal identification as much of his filmmaking and writing, they still reflect many of the themes, both psychological and mythic, found in his work in those media.

The interviews and essays contained in this collection encompass the artistic journey that Ingmar Bergman embarked upon in the mid-forties and continues to make today. This journey has lasted half a century, but Bergman continues to explore, with the restless curiosity of youth, the pain of existence and the wonder of art and the myriad ways the two constantly intersect with and enrich each other.

—Roger W. Oliver

PART ONE

BERGMAN ON BERGMAN

EACH FILM IS MY LAST

INGMAR BERGMAN

During the 1950s Ingmar Bergman was often asked to articulate his approach to filmmaking. The following essay, edited by Erika Munk for the fall 1966 issue of the Drama Review, *is drawn from two speeches that Bergman made for Svensk Filmindustri, where his films were produced at that time.*

I COMPARE ARTISTIC CREATION TO HUNGER. I ACKNOWLedged it with a certain satisfaction, but during my conscious life I never asked myself what caused this craving. In the last few years the hunger has diminished and been transformed into something else; now I am anxious to find out what the reasons for it were. I have early childhood memories of my desire to show off achievements: proficiency in drawing, in playing ball, the first swimmingstrokes. I had a strong need to draw the grown-ups' attention to these signs of my presence in the external world. I never felt that people took enough interest in me. When reality was no longer sufficient, I started to invent things: I entertained my friends with tremendous stories of my secret exploits. They were embarrassing lies, which failed hopelessly when confronted with the levelheaded skepticism of the world around me. Finally I withdrew, and kept my dream world to myself. A child looking for human contact, obsessed by his imagination, had been quickly transformed into a hurt, cunning, and suspicious daydreamer.

But a daydreamer is no artist except in his dreams.

The need to be heard, to correspond, to live in the warmth of a community, was still there. It grew stronger the lonelier I grew. It goes without saying that film became my means of expression. I made myself understood in a language beyond words, which failed me; beyond music, which I did not master; beyond painting, which left me indifferent. I was suddenly able to correspond with the world around me in a language spoken literally from soul to soul, in phrases which escaped the control of the intellect in an almost voluptuous way. With the total stunted hunger of a child I seized upon my medium and for twenty years, tirelessly and in a kind of frenzy, I supplied the world with dreams, intellectual excitement, fantasies, fits of lunacy. My success has been amazing, but at bottom it is an insignificant sequel.

I do not underestimate what I may have achieved. I think that it has been and perhaps still is of importance. But now I can see the past in a

new and less romantic light; that is security enough for me. Today my situation is less complicated, less interesting, above all less glamorous than it was. To be completely frank, I experience art (not only film art) as insignificant in our time: art no longer has the power and the possibility to influence the development of our life.

Literature, painting, music, film, and theater beget and bring forth themselves. New mutations, new combinations arise and are annihilated; the movement seems — seen from the outside — nervously vital. With magnificent zeal the artists project to themselves and to a more and more distracted public pictures of a world that no longer cares what they like or think. In a few countries artists are punished, art is considered dangerous and worth stifling and directing. On the whole, however, art is free, shameless, irresponsible; the movement is intense, almost feverish, like a snake's skin full of ants. The snake is long since dead, eaten, deprived of his poison, but the skin is full of meddlesome life.

If I have become one of these ants, I must ask myself if there is any reason to continue my work.

The answer is yes. Although I think that the stage is an old, beloved kept woman, who has seen better days. Although I and many other people find the Wild West more stimulating than Antonioni and Bergman. Although the new music gives us the sense of being suffocated by mathematically rarefied air. Although painting and sculpture, sterilized, decline in their own paralyzing freedom. Although literature has been transformed into a pile of words without any message or dangerous qualities.

I think that people today can dispense with theater because they exist in the middle of a drama whose different phases incessantly produce local tragedies. They do not need music because every minute they are exposed to hurricanes of sound passing beyond endurance. They do not need poetry because the idea of the universe has transformed them into functional animals, confined to interesting — but from a poetical point of view unusable — problems of metabolic disturbance. Man (as I experience myself and the world around me) has made himself free, terribly and dizzyingly free. Religion and art are kept alive as conventional politeness toward the past, as benign, democratic solicitude on behalf of nervous citizens enjoying more and more leisure time.

If I consider all these troubles and still maintain that I want to continue to work in art, there is a simple reason. (I disregard the purely material one.) The reason is *curiosity*. A boundless, insatiable curiosity that is always new and that pushes me onward — a curiosity that never leaves me alone and that has completely replaced my craving for community. I feel like a prisoner who, after serving a long term, suddenly is confronted with turbulent life. I note, I observe, I keep my eyes open; everything is unreal, fantastic, frightening, or ridiculous. I catch a flying grain of dust; maybe it is a film — what importance does it have? None at all, but I find it interesting and consequently it is a film. I walk around with the grain of dust that I have caught in my own hand. I am happy or sad. I jostle the other ants; together we accomplish an enormous task. The snake's skin moves.

This and only this is *my* truth. I do not require that it be valid for someone else, and as a consolation for eternity it is of course rather meager. As a basis for artistic activity during future years it is completely sufficient, at least for me. To devote oneself to artistic creation for one's own satisfaction is not always agreeable. But it has one great advantage: the artist lives exactly like every other living creature that exists only for its own sake. This makes a rather numerous brotherhood.

Experience should be gained before one reaches forty, a wise man said. After forty it is

The young Ingmar Bergman on location

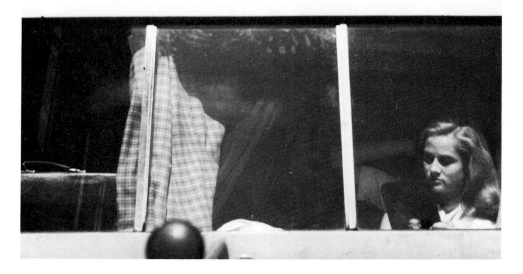

Bergman directing his first film, Crisis *(1945) with cinematographer Gösta Roosling*

permissible to comment. The reverse might apply in my case. No one was more certain of his theories and none more willing to elucidate them than I was. No one knew better or could visualize more. Now that I am older I have become rather more cautious. The experience I have gained and which I am now sorting out is such that I am unwilling to express myself on the art of the filmmaker. . . . The only real contribution the artist can make is his work. Thus I find it rather unseemly to get involved in discussions, explanations, or excuses.

In an earlier time, the fact that the artist often remained unknown was a good thing. His relative anonymity was a guarantee against irrelevant outside influences, material considerations, and the prostitution of his talents. He brought forth his work in spirit and truth as he saw it and left the judgment to the Lord. Thus he lived and died without being more or less important than any other artisan. In such a world natural assurance and invulnerable humility flourished, two qualities that are the finest hallmarks of art.

In life today, the position of the artist has become more and more precarious: the artist has become a curious figure, a kind of performer or athlete who chases from job to job. His isolation, his now almost holy individualism, his artistic subjectivity can all too easily cause ulcers and neurosis. Exclusiveness becomes a curse he eulogizes. The unusual is both his pain and his satisfaction. . . .

The script often begins with something very hazy and indefinite — a chance remark or a quick change of phrase, a dim but pleasant event that is not specifically related to the actual situation. It has happened in my theatrical work that I visualize performers in fresh makeup but in yet-unplayed roles. Often these are mere split-second impressions that disappear as quickly as they come, forming a brightly colored thread sticking out in the dark sack of the unconscious. If I wind up this thread carefully, a complete film will emerge, brought out with pulsebeats and rhythms characteristic of that film. Through these rhythms the picture sequences take on patterns, according to their early inspirations.

The feeling of failure occurs mostly before the writing begins. The dreams turn into cobwebs, the visions fade and become gray and insignificant, the pulsebeat is silent, everything shrinks into tired fancies without strength and reality. But I have decided to start a certain film, and the hard work must begin: to transfer rhythms, moods, atmosphere, tensions, sequences, tones, and scents into a readable or at least understandable script.

This is difficult but not impossible.

The vital element is the dialogue, but dialogue is a sensitive matter, which can offer resistance. The written dialogue of the theater is like a score that is almost incomprehensible to the ordinary person; interpretation demands a technical knack and a certain amount of imagination and feeling. One can write dialogue, but how it is to be handled — the rhythm and the tempo, the speed at which it is to be taken — and what is to take place between the lines — all that must be left out, because a script containing so much detail would be unreadable.

I can squeeze direction and location, characterizations and atmosphere into my film scripts in understandable terms. The essentials follow, by which I mean, montage, rhythm, and the relation of one frame to the other — the vital "third dimension" without which the film is merely dead. Here I cannot use "keys" or show an adequate indication of the tempos of the complexes involved; it is impossible to give a comprehensible notion of what puts life into a work of art. I have often sought a kind of notation that would give me a chance of recording the shadings and tones of the ideas and the inner structure of the picture. If I could express myself clearly with this, I could work with the absolute certainty that whenever I liked I could prove the relationship between rhythm and continuity of the part and the whole. . . . Let us state once and for all that the film script is a very imperfect *technical* basis for a film.

Film is not like literature. More often than not the character and substance of the two art forms are in conflict. The written word is read and assimilated by a conscious act and in connection with the intellect, and little by little it plays on the imagination or feelings. It is completely different with the motion picture. When we see a film in a cinema we are conscious that an illusion has been prepared for us and we relax and accept it with our will and intellect. We prepare the way into our imagination. The sequence of images plays directly on our feelings without touching our mind.

There are many reasons why we ought to avoid filming existing literature, but the most important is that the intangible dimension, which is the heart of a literary work, is often untranslatable, and that in its turn kills the special dimension of the film. If, despite this, we wish to translate something literary into filmic terms, we are obliged to make an infinite number of complicated transformations which most often give limited or nonexistent results in relation to the efforts expended. I know what I am talking about because I have been subjected to so-called literary judgment. This is like letting a music critic judge an art exhibition or a football reporter criticize a new stage play. The only reason for everyone believing himself capable of pronouncing a valid judgment on motion pictures is the inability of the film to assert itself as an art form, its need of a definite artistic vocabulary, its extreme youth in relation to the other arts, its obvious ties with economic realities, its direct appeal to the feelings. All these cause film to be regarded with disdain. Its directness of expression makes it suspect in certain eyes, and as a result any and everyone thinks he's competent to say anything he likes, in whatever way he likes, about film art.

I myself have never had ambitions to be an author. I do not wish to write novels, short stories, essays, biographies, or treatises on special subjects. I certainly do not want to write pieces for the theater. Filmmaking is what interests me. I want to make films about conditions, tensions, pictures, rhythms, and characters that have a special interest to me. The motion picture and its complicated process of birth are my methods of expressing my quests and needs to my fellow men. It irritates me that a work is judged as a book when it is a film. Consequently the writing of the script is a difficult period, but useful, because it compels me to prove logically the validity of my ideas. While this is taking place I am caught in a difficult conflict between my need to find a way of filming a complicated situation and my desire for complete simplicity. Since I do not intend my work to be solely for my own edification or for a happy few, but for the public at large, meeting the demands of the public is imperative. Sometimes I try a venturesome alternative, which shows that the public can appreciate the most advanced and complicated developments. . . .

I stand in the half-light of the film studio with its noise and crowds, dirt and wretched atmosphere, and I always ask myself why I am engaged in this most difficult form of artistic creation. The rules are many and burdensome. I must achieve three minutes of usable film in the can every day. I must keep to the shooting schedule, which is so tight that it excludes almost everything but essentials. I am surrounded by technical equipment, which with fiendish cunning tries to sabotage my best intentions. Constantly I am on edge, I am compelled to live the collective life of the studio. Out of all this must emerge a sensitive process, which demands quiet, concentration, and confidence.

I mean working with actors and actresses. There are many directors who forget that our

Bergman reviewing scenes with Signe Hasso and Alf Kjellin during the filming of This Can't Happen Here *(1950)*

work in films begins with the human face. We certainly can become completely absorbed in the aesthetics of montage, we can bring objects and still life into a wonderful rhythm together, we can make nature studies of astounding beauty, but the approach to the human face is without doubt the distinguishing quality of the film. From this we might conclude that the film star is our most expensive instrument and the camera only registers the reactions of this instrument. But in many cases the position and movement of the camera is considered more important than the player, and the picture becomes an end in itself. This can never do anything but destroy illusions and be artistically devastating. In order to give the greatest possible strength to the actor's expression, the camera movement must be simple, free, and completely synchronized with the action. The camera must be an objective observer and may only on rare occasions participate in the action. We should realize that the best means of expression the actor has at his command is his *look*. The close-up, if objectively composed, perfectly directed and played, is the most forcible means at the disposal of the film director, while at the same time it is the most certain proof of his competence or incompetence. The lack or abundance of close-ups shows in an uncompromising way the nature of the director and the extent of his interest in people.

Simplicity, concentration, full knowledge, technical perfection must be the pillars supporting each scene and sequence. However, they in themselves are not enough. The most important thing is still lacking: the intimate spark of life, which appears or fails to appear according to its will, crucial and indomitable.

For instance, everything for each scene must be prepared down to the last detail; each member of the film crew must know exactly what he or she is to do. The entire mechanism must be free from fault as a matter of course. These preliminaries may or may not take a long time. Rehearsals for the "take" must be carried out with technical precision and, again, with everyone knowing exactly what he or she is to do. Then comes the take. From experience I know that the first take is often the happiest, because it is the most natural. At that moment the actors are focusing on creating something, and their creative urge comes from identification with their parts. The camera registers this inner act of creation, which is hardly perceptible to the untrained eye or ear. I believe it is this very moment that keeps me in films. The development and retention of a sudden burst of life gives me ample reward for the thousands of hours of gray gloom, trial, and tribulation. . . .

Many imagine that the commercial film industry lacks morality or that its morals are so definitely based on immorality that an artistically ethical standpoint cannot be maintained. Our work is assigned to businessmen, who often regard it with apprehension because it is concerned with something as unreliable as art. If many regard our activity as dubious, I must emphasize that its morality is as good as any and so absolute that it is almost embarrassing. However, I have found that I am like the Englishman in the tropics who shaves and dresses for dinner every day. He obviously does not dress to please the wild animals, but for his own sake. If he gives up his discipline, then the jungle has beaten him. I know that I shall have lost to the jungle if I take a weak moral standpoint. I have therefore come to a belief based on three commandments. I shall attempt to give their wording and their meaning. These have become the basis of my activity in the film world.

The first may sound indecent, but it is really highly moral:

THOU SHALT BE ENTERTAINING AT ALL TIMES

The public who sees my films and thus provides for my existence has the right to expect entertainment, a thrill, joy, a spirited experience. I am responsible for providing that experience. That is the only justification for my activity.

Yet, this does not mean that I must prostitute my talents, which leads me to my second commandment:

THOU SHALT OBEY
THY ARTISTIC CONSCIENCE AT ALL TIMES

This is a very tricky commandment, because it obviously forbids me to steal, lie, prostitute my talents, kill, or falsify. However, I will say that I am allowed to falsify if it is artistically justified; I may also lie if it is a beautiful lie; I could also kill my friends or myself or anyone else if it would help my art; it may also be permissible to prostitute my talents if it will further my cause, and I should indeed steal if there were no other way out. If I obeyed my artistic conscience to the full in every respect, I would be doing a balancing act on a tightrope, and could become so dizzy that at any moment I could break my neck. Then all the prudent and moral bystanders would say, "Look, there lies the thief, the murderer, the lecher, the liar. Serves him right" — never thinking that all means are allowed except those that lead to a fiasco, and that the most dangerous ways are the only ones that are passable, and that compulsion and dizziness are two necessary parts of our activity; that the joy of creation, which is a thing of beauty and joy forever, is bound up with the necessary fear of creation. . . .

In order to strengthen my will so that I do not slip off the narrow path into the ditch, I have a third commandment:

THOU SHALT MAKE EACH FILM
AS IF IT WERE THY LAST

Some may imagine that this commandment is an amusing paradox or a pointless aphorism or perhaps simply an empty and beautiful phrase about the complete vanity of everything. That is not the case.

It is reality.

In Sweden, film production was halted for all of 1951. During this enforced inactivity I learned that because of commercial complications and through no fault of my own I could be out on the street, unemployed. I do not complain about it, neither am I afraid or bitter; I have only drawn a logical and highly moral conclusion from the situation: *Each film is my last.*

For me there is only one loyalty: to the film on which I am working. What comes (or fails to come) after is insignificant and causes neither anxiety nor longing. This gives me assurance and artistic confidence. The material assurance is apparently limited, but I find artistic integrity infinitely more important, and therefore I follow the principle that *each film is my last.* This gives me strength in another way. I have seen all too many filmmakers burdened with anxiety, yet carrying out to the full their necessary duties. Worn out, bored to death, and without pleasure, they have fulfilled their work. They have suffered humiliation and affronts from producers, critics, and the public without flinching, without giving up, without leaving the profession. With a tired shrug of the shoulders they have made their artistic contributions until they gave up or were thrown out.

The day might come when I am received indifferently by the public. That day I will, perhaps, be disgusted with myself. Tiredness and emptiness will descend upon me like a dirty gray sack, and fear will stifle everything. Emptiness will stare me in the face. When this happens I shall put down my tools and leave the scene, of my own free will, without bitterness and without brooding about whether the work has been useful and truthful from the viewpoint of eternity. Wise and farsighted men in the Middle Ages used to spend nights in their coffins in order never to forget the tremendous importance of every moment and the transient nature of life itself. Without taking such a drastic and uncomfortable measure, I harden myself against the seeming futility and the fickle cruelty of filmmaking with the earnest conviction that *each film is my last.*

Translated by Erika Munk

REMEMBERING ALF SJÖBERG

INGMAR BERGMAN

Although there were many important influences on Ingmar Bergman's career as a theater and film director, one of the most significant was that of Alf Sjöberg. The first production Bergman saw at the Royal Dramatic Theater (Dramaten) was directed by Sjöberg, who years later directed Bergman's first produced screenplay. When Bergman became director of the Dramaten, he was in the unusual position of being the older director's supervisor.

ALF SJÖBERG HAD CHOSEN TALL YOUNG WOMEN FOR THE chorus in *Alcestis,* among them the promising Margaretha Byström, who had just graduated from our drama school. Another director wanted her in a major part. As Director of the Theater, I arbitrarily transferred her, without asking Sjöberg; the decision was approved, and the cast list pinned on the notice board. A few hours later, a roaring sound penetrated right through the double doors and thundered through the thick walls of my office. A crash and a bellow followed. In came Alf Sjöberg, white with rage, demanding that I immediately reinstate Margaretha Byström. It was impossible, I replied, the other production would give her a real chance at last. I also added that I did not give way to bullying. In disbelief, Sjöberg threatened to punch me. Retreating behind the board table I mumbled something about bloody peasant manners. The furious Sjöberg yelled that he always knew that I had worked against him since the very first day, and the limit had now been reached. Coming around the table, I went up to him, daring him to hit me. I managed a frightened smile. Sjöberg's face was trembling,

his whole body shaking, and both of us were breathing heavily. We both realized how absurd the situation was.

Sjöberg sat down on the nearest chair and asked how two relatively well-brought-up men could behave so idiotically. I promised I would give him back Margaretha Byström. With a dismissive gesture he left the room. We never mentioned the matter again. Our relationship seemed peppered with violent disagreements, both artistic and personal, but we always managed to treat each other with courtesy and without rancor.

I had attended the Royal Dramatic Theater for the first time in my life at Christmas in 1930. They were doing Geijerstam's fairy-tale play *Big Klas and Little Klas.* The producer was Alf Sjöberg, then twenty-seven years old, and it was his second production. I remember every detail, the lights, the set, the sunrise over the small elves in national costume, the boat on the river, the old church with St. Peter as doorkeeper, the cross-section of the house. I was sitting in the second row of the upper circle, nearest to the exit door.

Years later, in the quiet hour at the theater between rehearsals and the evening performance, I would occasionally sit in my old seat and give in to nostalgia, feeling that this impractical and faded place was really my home. This imposing auditorium lying in silence and semidarkness was — I must write after great hesitation — "the beginning and the end and almost everything in between." If it looks silly and exaggerated in print, I can't find a better way of putting it — the beginning and the end and almost everything in between.

Alf Sjöberg never needed a ruler when he had to measure stage surfaces and draw a sketch of a scene. His hand knew the exact scale.

So he stayed on at the Dramaten after his debut as a passionate young actor. His teacher, Maria Schildknecht, said: "He was a very gifted young actor, but he was so damned lazy he became a director." He remained in that same theater until he died, except for two or three times when he was a guest director at other theaters. He lingered on at the Dramaten and became its prince and prisoner. I don't think I've ever met anyone with such violent contradictions within himself. His face was a marionette's mask, controlled by will and ruthless charm. Behind that determined façade, social insecurity, intellectual passion, self-knowledge, self-deception, courage and cowardice, black humor and deadly seriousness, gentleness and brutality, impatience and endless patience either fought each other or blended in harmony. Like all producers, he also acted the part of a producer; since he was a gifted actor, the performance was convincing.

I never tried to compete with Sjöberg. In the theater he was my superior. His interpretations of Shakespeare covered everything, and I had nothing else to add. He knew more than I did and looked more deeply, then re-created what he saw.

His generosity often gave rise to mean and petty-minded criticism. I had no idea at the time that he was hurt by such gray whimpering.

He was probably most deeply affected by our provincial cultural revolution during the international wave of student unrest. Unlike me, Sjöberg was politically committed and spoke pas-sionately about theater as a weapon. When the movement blew in over the Dramaten, he wanted to man the barricades with the young. His bitterness was great when he found himself reading that the Dramaten should be burned to the ground, that Sjöberg and Bergman should be hanged from the Tornberg clock in Nybroplan.

It is possible some brave researcher will one day investigate just how much damage was done to our cultural life by the 1968 movement. It is possible, but hardly likely. Today, frustrated revolutionaries still cling to their desks in editorial offices and talk bitterly about "the renewal that stopped short." They do not see (and how could they!) that their contribution was a deadly slashing blow at an evolution that must never be separated from its roots. In other countries, where varied ideas are allowed to flourish at the same time, tradition and education were not destroyed. Only in China and Sweden were artists and teachers scorned.

I myself, under the eyes of my own son, was driven out of the state drama school. When I maintained that young students had to learn their trade to enable them to go out with their revolutionary message, they waved the "little red book" and whistled, ingratiatingly cheered on by Niklas Brunius, the principal of the school at the time.

The young rapidly and skillfully organized themselves, attracted the mass media, and left us, the old and exhausted, in cruel isolation. I personally was not really obstructed in my work. My public was in other countries and earned me a living as well as keeping me in a good mood. Yet I despised a fanaticism I recognized from my childhood, the same emotional sludge, only the content different. Instead of fresh air, we had distortion, sectarianism, intolerance, anxious toadying, and a misuse of power. The pattern is unchanging: ideas become institutionalized and corrupted. Sometimes it happens quickly, sometimes it takes hundreds of years. In 1968, it happened at furious speed, and the damage done in a short time was both astonishing and hard to repair.

During his last years, Alf Sjöberg did several great things. He translated and adapted Claudel's

Alf Sjöberg (center) directing a scene from Bergman's screenplay Torment *(1944)*

The Annunciation to Mary, an imperishable performance. He put on Brecht's *Galileo* [*Das Leben des Galilei*], constructed with massive blocks. And last, he directed a *School for Wives* that was playful, reserved, and unsentimental.

We had rooms off the same corridor outside the upper circle and often met hurrying to or from rehearsals or meetings. Sometimes we sat down on rickety wooden chairs and talked, gossiped, or complained. We seldom went further and never met privately, but simply sat on wooden chairs, sometimes for several hours. It became a ritual.

Years later, as I still hurry to my room along that same windowless, reeking, dimly lit corridor, I daydream that perhaps we'll run into each other.

Translated by Joan Tate

BERGMAN'S BEST INTENTIONS

LASSE BERGSTRÖM

Lasse Bergström has been for nearly three decades the editor-in-chief of the Swedish publishing house Norstedts Förlag, Ingmar Bergman's Swedish publisher. A critic, Bergström has also been one of Bergman's closest friends.

AT SEVENTY-FOUR INGMAR BERGMAN IS ONE OF THE world's greatest living filmmakers, a creative genius whose magic touch also extends to theater, opera, and television. But he is also a most private, even secretive, man and over the years has learned to protect his privacy. He grants almost no interviews.

My own, exceptional, opportunities to speak with him, on the record, were the result of a long professional relationship and, with time, friendship. When we first met, nearly forty years ago, it was across a barricade: he a filmmaker, I a critic. His suspicion was understandable. He had been so hounded by critics in his native Sweden that, for a time, he even refused to publish the scripts of his films there. In the early 1960s I became his publisher; the relationship has endured and deepened.

A few years ago, we sat down at his home on Fårö, a Baltic island retreat much favored by the Swedish cultural elite, and the setting for several of Bergman's films. Altogether, our conversations went on for more than fifty hours, forming the basis for Bergman's book *Bilder,* published in English as *Images: My Life in Film.* Later, we met again on Fårö. The following interview is the result of that meeting.

Fårö is Ingmar Bergman's private kingdom, his earthly paradise. He has lived there in seclusion for nearly a quarter of a century. The house is shrouded in foliage and nearly invisible, at the edge of a low forest and above a desolate, stony beach. Even after his arrest and humiliation at the hands of the Swedish tax authorities, when he left Sweden for voluntary exile in Munich, he was unable to give up Fårö.

"I can understand why people might think it strange for someone to suddenly decide to live on an island he'd never even heard of before," he admitted.

"How did that come about?" I asked him.

"I was about to make *Through a Glass Darkly* in 1960. It is set on an island, with four people who rise up from a twilight sea in the first scene and walk ashore to begin the drama. I had this idea that we would do the film in the Orkney Islands.

"The Orkneys were out of the question, for

reasons of cost, and after a few fruitless excursions in the Stockholm archipelago someone asked me if I'd ever seen Fårö."

BERGSTRÖM: Was it love at first sight?

BERGMAN: I was enthralled, gripped by a strange fascination. Between takes we wandered around the island and when I returned a few years later for *Persona,* I suddenly felt: This is where I want to live!

BERGSTRÖM: Can you explain why?

BERGMAN: Yes, in part. It's the never-ceasing sounds of the wind, the waves, the gulls. The enormity of the sea creates a sense of timelessness, changelessness, security. But it's also the proportions and ancient character of the landscape. There isn't a whole lot of leafy foliage, not a whole lot of sandy beach, cliffs, and rocks, and not a whole lot of woods. But there is something of it all here in a kind of wonderful balance and harmony — the low stone walls running through the flat landscape, which can appear harsh and drab, only to suddenly blossom after the spring melt in vast carpets of color and life. And then there's the light. I can sit for hours just looking out the window, watching how the light wanders and shifts.

At this time, Bergman was already working hard to prepare *The Bacchae,* his first production at the Stockholm Opera since Stravinsky's *The Rake's Progress* in 1961. He had come to Fårö directly after a big hit with *Peer Gynt.* From Fårö, he kept himself informed about the tour to New York of three other productions he had staged in Stockholm: *Long Day's Journey Into Night, A Doll's House,* and *Miss Julie.* Meanwhile, he was also proofreading his latest book, *Den goda viljan (The Best Intentions),* a novel based on his parents' youth and early marriage. Bille August's film version of *The Best Intentions,* Swedish television's most ambitious project to that date, was the big hit of the Christmas TV season in Sweden in 1991. A shorter, feature-length version had its international premiere at the 1992 Cannes Film Festival.

Börje Ahlstedt and Solveig Ternström in Ibsen's Peer Gynt *at the Royal Dramatic Theater of Sweden in 1991, presented at the Brooklyn Academy of Music in 1993*

BERGSTRÖM: For an old man sitting by the sea, you have an unusually heavy work load. Don't you think it will soon be time to take leave of the theater, as you have already done with film?

BERGMAN: I will. It's absolutely necessary. I look forward to enjoying what I perceive to be absolute freedom, which is being able to sit here in my chair at any hour of the day and read a book I think is fun to read. Or a heavy tome that is hard work to read, and requires me to think over what I've read, underline, and make notes. And then enjoy a movie, take a walk, read the newspaper, and do some writing. As stimulating and enjoyable as it is to work with theater, there is a demand implied in the work which is beginning to weigh heavily on me.

BERGSTRÖM: Recently, you've been involved in very large productions, such as *Peer Gynt,* and now the new opera version of *The Bacchae.*

BERGMAN: That's right. But, nowadays, I only do things I think are fun. I've done far too much theater in my life for rational, logical, or economic reasons. Because it's been important for the Royal Dramatic Theater in Stockholm, or for one actor or another.

BERGSTRÖM: Is there any halfway position? You once told me you planned to conclude your theatrical career with some small performances on lesser stages, with a few young, beautiful actresses.

BERGMAN: There is a big advantage to having worked so many years in the theater. When I was young, experience was a highly valued commodity. Those who had been in the profession for many years and had much to teach were greatly sought after. This attitude has been absent for many years, since zero value has been attached to tradition, insight, and knowledge. Now, people with knowledge and experience — even though they may be old and tired — are once again sought after to help young actors. People have grown tired of woolly-mindedness.

BERGSTRÖM: Is this an area where you feel you have something to give?

BERGMAN: I don't mean to set up some kind of program. But I think it's fun to be with young people and see that they are making use of me as a resource.

BERGSTRÖM: You're referring primarily to the actors?

BERGMAN: I'm talking only about them. No one else.

BERGSTRÖM: Isn't there any similar passing-on of experience and tradition from you to young directors in the theater?

BERGMAN: No, I don't think so. There are young directors who think it's nice to have me around. They nod politely and look interested, but I don't believe for a moment I can be of any use to them.

BERGSTRÖM: When we were working on *Images: My Life in Film,* we talked about how the 1968 student movement, viewed retrospectively, wreaked so much havoc in so many cultural fields. Was this due to woolly-mindedness?

BERGMAN: The theater was damaged in a devastating way. With film, market forces were still in control, but in government-subsidized theaters — and schools — there was a kind of cultural revolution that left nothing intact.

BERGSTRÖM: In the literary field, it could be said, with some exaggeration, that we lost a whole generation of poets and storytellers.

BERGMAN: I think that, today, outside the Royal Dramatic Theater, we have adult actors who could have been great thespians, bearers of tradition, but who suffered greatly due to a lack of instruction, and have, therefore, never come into contact with their true artistic identities.

BERGSTRÖM: There was an attempt to suppress the classics, wasn't there?

BERGMAN: Above all, the classics weren't to be played as classics. They had to be rewritten or butchered, reduced to public polemics or private confrontations. They were dismantled and disarmed. Instead of showing the unadulterated classics in all their explosive energy, an effort was made to reduce them to something cut and dried, clear and concise, easy to comprehend.

Börje Ahlstedt as Peer Gynt at the Royal Dramatic Theater of Sweden in 1991, presented at the Brooklyn Academy of Music in 1993

BERGSTRÖM: Since you came back from Germany, you have gone in for demonstrating the power in these classics again.

BERGMAN: I'm certainly not alone in that. There is a trend now to put on plays the way they are written, without trying to change them beyond recognition. But it took a long time to come around to this. A couple of decades.

BERGSTRÖM: The enormous success of *Peer Gynt,* with both critics and audiences, must please you immensely.

BERGMAN: Yes, but it isn't quite as fantastic as when, on returning to the Royal Dramatic Theater, I staged a production of Shakespeare's *King Lear* that ran to over a hundred full houses. It has never been a public favorite.

When Bergman did his first *Peer Gynt,* in Malmö in 1957, it was played almost uncut, running to about five hours, but in his latest production of this play he has cut it by about twenty percent.

BERGSTRÖM: Now, *Peer Gynt*'s been staged with careful judgment, well thought out, not like in Malmö, where you simply did the whole thing as it was written.

BERGMAN: I suppose that's a symptom of age. Even playful works like this one have to be well thought out. To keep the rehearsals from getting tedious, it is necessary to give careful thought even to whims, gimmicks, and spectacular scenes.

BERGSTRÖM: I imagine it must feel tedious to start work on a production, but that the tedium turns to fun as rehearsals progress.

BERGMAN: It's actually the other way around. The fun part is in the conception. The playfulness, the dreaming, the fun and games are in the notebooks — the wonderful feeling of total freedom, that you can do anything you want. Then, when you have to codify this in contact with the script and the actors, that's when it's important to keep the fun from turning to tedium. You have to re-create it with painstaking care and attention to detail. I have to sit at my desk at home and draw scenery and try to transform what I thought was fun and fanciful into boring arrows and figures. Then this, in turn, has to be communicated to the actors and tap into their creativity, so that they, too, feel all the freedom, fun, and joy. For me, theatrical work has always been broken down into a fun period, when the time flies, and a dull, pedantic period.

BERGSTRÖM: Does the pedantic period cast its shadow over the fun period and spoil it?

BERGMAN: No, they're so divorced from each other. Then, there is a tremendous sense of satisfaction when I see that the actors are enjoying their work. When we get warm contact during the rehearsals, when they look eagerly at me because they sense we're on the same wavelength, on the same track. Then I feel that all the boring, hard work I've put into my direction books has been worthwhile.

In Bergman's production of *The Bacchae*, he has been careful to give members of the chorus individual faces instead of the anonymous masks that are the convention in ancient tragedy. He sees the chorus as a group of terrorists held together by the cult of Dionysus, now assembled in Thebes to take part in the cruel plot.

He has gone so far as to give each of them a name and life history, following in his imagination their journeys to Thebes right across the map of the ancient world, from as far afield as present-day Afghanistan and Pakistan. These stories will play no part in the action, but Bergman's intention is that they should influence the character portrayals.

BERGSTRÖM: We spoke earlier of absolute freedom. You have, undeniably, a nice opportunity now to write freely.

BERGMAN: I sometimes think of Lampedusa, who wrote *The Leopard*. He was an old Sicilian nobleman who lived in his somewhat dilapidated villa. Every morning, he took his briefcase and plodded down all the stairs to the trattoria on the corner. There he had his table,

there he drank his espresso or whatever, and there he sat writing until lunch. Thus he passed the days, producing thousands of pages of manuscript. He apparently had no intention of publishing anything. For me, there is something fascinating about this, since throughout my whole life and career I have always worked with an audience in mind. Now, I'm looking forward to the summer. From May until Christmas I intend to sit here on Fårö and write just for the fun of it. It's a new feeling: I don't have to worry about whether it will be heard, seen, or shown.

BERGSTRÖM: But is this just another kind of artistic activity, alone in a room away from the big artistic machineries that otherwise keep you occupied?

BERGMAN: I have always envied my writer friends when they say: "I don't think I'll finish my novel this year. I think I'll need another year." What a wonderful sense of timelessness! Lampedusa was undoubtedly a happy man. For me, now able to live here on Fårö like an aging country gentleman, with a somewhat stormy life behind me, it's a delight to settle down to a peaceful existence in which I can write page after page here at my desk, taking pure enjoyment in letting my hand go. My sole audience and reader will be my wife, Ingrid, which is really quite enough for me.

BERGSTRÖM: There are many people who say that a text is meaningful as long it has a single reader.

BERGMAN: I already feel great contentment today when I answer all the mail I get as a filmmaker. I can say quite honestly: "I'm sorry, but I've retired. I can't regard myself as being involved. Thank you for the honor, but I don't have time. I don't want to, I'm not playing the game anymore."

BERGSTRÖM: There's a curious aspect of *The Best Intentions* in relation to your autobiography, *The Magic Lantern*. You wanted to correct the picture of your parents, understand something that wasn't clear even when you wrote your autobiography.

BERGMAN: It's an even longer process than that. I

Jarl Kulle (center) and cast members of King Lear *at the Royal Dramatic Theater of Sweden in 1984*

started to come to terms with Mother and Father while they were still alive. For many years, my relationship to my parents had been very neurotic, a terrible business, with a great deal of hate and misunderstanding. My whole life-style, my whole way of existing and grabbing what I could in life, frightened both Mother and Father, since they had always lived under strict ethical laws. The only thing we had in common was that, ever since childhood, I had been plagued by a terrible sense of duty. That was one thing they had really succeeded in instilling in me, and it's still solidly in place.

BERGSTRÖM: Maybe it's not such a bad legacy?

BERGMAN: For someone like me, who has a some-what hysterical disposition, with a constant need to run away and pull a blanket over my head, the whip in the flesh is undoubtedly a good thing. You must never run away, you must never try to shirk your responsibility. My parents taught me that in blood. But the picture of my parents that emerged publicly from everything that was written in biographies and articles about my unhappy childhood and my horrible father — it wasn't true. My childhood was difficult in many ways, but it was also colorful and rich. I was never bored.

BERGSTRÖM: But it was the dark side that came out in your films?

BERGMAN: Yes, that was the visible side, the hellishness of bourgeois life and all that. But then I wrote *The Magic Lantern* and started to get another picture of Mother and Father. One day, while watching a Swedish TV series, I started thinking about a subject for a TV series of my own, encouraged by the fun I had had writing *Scenes from a Marriage,* an earlier series I had done. The first thing that came to mind was this business of Mother and Father, which I had been pondering for a long time. I had looked at photographs from their youth and started to put together what I knew. It was like jumping from one ice floe to the next. Some things Father had told me, some things Mother had told me, and a little I got from the family chronicle. Then when it started to come together it turned into quite a drama. At the end of *The Magic Lantern,* I have a chapter in which I visit Mother after her death. Afterward I didn't think it turned out so well. I just couldn't make it work, simply because I lacked a deep enough understanding. Today, I would be able to write that chapter much more successfully. Now, I have access to my mother's diaries, and, be-sides, I've written *The Best Intentions* — I know and I feel so much more.

It was truly a pleasure to delve into all of this and write about it. And during the course of the work, I felt I began to get to know my parents, their ambitions and their helplessness, their competence, their kindness, their anger, and their jealousy. I started to see them as two living human beings. It may be because I am very much a half-and-half product of Mother and Father. It's almost absurd how much like both of them I am. And I'm sure you can understand that, after this, every form of reproach, blame, bitterness, or even vague feeling that they have messed up my life is gone forever from my mind.

BERGSTRÖM: That must be a great relief.

BERGMAN: It is a blessing. My brother died unre-conciled. My sister is still raging. I am privi-leged.

Translated by Richard E. Nord

PART TWO

DIRECTORS ON BERGMAN

Through a Life Darkly

WOODY ALLEN

Woody Allen, one of America's foremost filmmakers, has long written and spoken of his admiration for Ingmar Bergman. Among Allen's many films are Love and Death, Annie Hall, Manhattan, Interiors, Hannah and Her Sisters, *and* Bullets Over Broadway. *This review of Bergman's book of memoirs,* The Magic Lantern, *first appeared in the* New York Times Book Review *in 1988.*

THE VOICE OF GENIUS!

"Day after day I was dragged or carried, screaming with anguish, into the classroom. I vomited over everything I saw, fainted, and lost my sense of balance."

On mother: "I tried to embrace her and kiss her, but she pushed me away and slapped my face."

Father: "Brutal flogging was a recurrent argument." "He hit me and I hit him back. He staggered and ended up sitting on the floor." "Father had been taken to hospital and was to be operated on for a malignant tumour in his gullet. [Mother] wanted me to go to see him. I told her that I had neither time nor desire to do so."

On his brother: "My brother had scarlet fever. . . . (Naturally I hoped he would die. The disease was dangerous in those days.)" "When my brother opened the door, I crashed the carafe down on his head. The carafe shattered, my brother fell with blood pouring out of a gaping wound. A month or so later, he attacked me without warning and knocked out two of my front teeth. I responded by setting light to his bed when he was asleep."

Sister: "My elder brother and I, usually mortal enemies, made peace and planned various ways of killing this repulsive wretch."

On himself: "I have once or twice in my life toyed with the idea of committing suicide."

A religious household: "Most of our upbringing was based on such concepts as sin, confession, punishment, forgiveness, and grace. . . . This fact may well have contributed to our astonishing acceptance of Nazism."

And finally, summing up life: "You were born without purpose, you live without meaning. . . . When you die, you are extinguished."

With this kind of background one is forced to be a genius. Either that or you wind up giggling behind locked doors in a room the walls of which have been thickly upholstered by the state.

Less than ennobling was the motive for seeing my first Ingmar Bergman movie. The facts were these: I was a teenager living in Brooklyn, and word had got around that there was a Swedish film coming to our local foreign film house in which a young woman swam completely naked.

A scene from Illicit Interlude *(1950) with Maj-Britt Nilsson and Annalisa Ericson in the dressing-room mirror*

Rarely have I slept overnight on the curb to be the first on line for a movie, but when *Summer with Monika* opened at the Jewel in Flatbush, a young boy with red hair and black-rimmed glasses could be seen clubbing senior citizens to the floor in an effort to insure the choicest, unobstructed seat.

I never knew who directed the film nor did I care, nor was I sensitive at that age to the power of the work itself — the irony, the tensions, the German Expressionist style with its poetic black-and-white photography and its erotic sado-masochistic undertones. I came away reliving only the moment Harriet Andersson disrobed, and although it was my first exposure to a director who I would come to believe was pound for pound the best of all filmmakers, I did not know it then. It was

not until a few years after that, for want of something more stimulating than an evening of miniature golf, my date and I wandered in to catch a movie called *The Naked Night.* I was slightly older and beginning to take a greater interest in films, and the experience now was a decidedly more profound one. The German style was still the pervading influence and there was a gruesome, sadistic beating at the climax; although the story was not totally focused, the work was directed with such immense talent that I sat forward for an hour and a half, my eyes bulging. Indeed the sequence when Frost, the clown, goes to retrieve his whorish wife, who is splashing nude in the water to amuse some soldiers, was so masterful in its shot selection, editing rhythm, and inspired evocation of humiliation and pain that one has to go back to Eisenstein to find such moviemaking power. This time, by the way, I did note the director's name, which was Swedish and which I, as was usual for me then, filed and forgot.

Only in the late fifties, when I took my then wife to see a much talked about movie with the unpromising title *Wild Strawberries,* did I lock into what was to become a lifelong addiction to the films of Ingmar Bergman. I still recall my mouth dry and my heart pounding away from the first uncanny dream sequence to the last serene close-up. Who can forget such images? The clock with no hands. The horse-drawn hearse suddenly becoming stuck — the blinding sunlight and the face of the old man as he is being pulled into the coffin by his own dead body. Clearly here was a master with an inspired personal style; an artist of deep concern and intellect, whose films would prove equal to great European literature. Shortly after that I saw *The Magician,* an audacious black-and-white dramatization of certain Kierkegaardian ideas presented as an occult tale and spun out in an original, hypnotic camera style that reached its crescendo years later in the dreamlike *Cries and Whispers.* Lest the Kierkegaardian reference make the movie sound too dry or didactic, please be assured. *The Magician,* like most of Bergman's films, had one foot brilliantly planted in show business.

In addition to all else — and perhaps most important — Bergman is a great entertainer; a storyteller who never loses sight of the fact that no matter what ideas he's chosen to communicate, films are for exciting an audience. His theatricality is inspired. Such imaginative use of old-fashioned Gothic lighting, and stylish compositions. The flamboyant surrealism of the dreams and symbols. The opening montage of *Persona,* the dinner in *Hour of the Wolf,* and, in *The Passion of Anna,* the chutzpah to stop the engrossing story at intervals and let the actors explain to the audience what they are trying to do with their portrayals, are moments of showmanship at its best.

The Seventh Seal was always my favorite film, and I remember seeing it with a small audience at the old New Yorker Theater. Who would have thought that that subject matter could yield such a pleasurable experience? If I described the story and tried to persuade a friend to watch it with me, how far would I get? "Well," I'd say, "it takes place in plague-ridden medieval Sweden and explores the limits of faith and reason based on Danish — and some German — philosophical concepts." Now this is hardly anyone's idea of a good time, and yet it's all dealt off with such stupendous imagination, suspense, and flair that one sits riveted like a child at a harrowing fairy tale. Suddenly the black figure of Death appears on the seashore to claim his victim, and the Knight of Reason challenges him to a chess game, trying to stall for time and discover some meaning to life. The tale engages and stalks forward with sinister inevitability. Again, the images are breathtaking! The flagellants, the burning of the witch (worthy of Carl Dreyer), and the finale, as Death dances off with all the doomed people to the nether lands in one of the most memorable shots in all movies.

Bergman is prolific, and the films that followed these early works were rich and varied, as his obsession moved from God's silence to the tortured relations between anguished souls trying to make sense of their feelings. (Actually, the films described were not really early but middle works, because he had directed a number of movies, not seen here until after his style and reputation caught on. These earlier films are very good but surprisingly conventional, given where he was going.) His influences by the fifties had become well assimilated as his own genius took command. The Germans still impressed him. I see Fritz Lang in his work, and Carl Dreyer, the Dane. Also Chekhov, Strindberg, and Kafka. I divide his movies into ones that are merely superb (*Through a Glass Darkly, Winter Light, The Silence, The Virgin Spring, The Passion of Anna,* to name only some) and the truly remarkable masterpieces (*Persona, Cries and Whispers,* and *Scenes from a Marriage,* along with a few I discussed earlier). There are atypical ones like *Shame* and *Fanny and Alexander,* which provide their own special pleasures, and even an occasional stumble like *The Serpent's Egg* and *Face to Face.*

Yet always in Bergman's less successful experiments there are memorable moments. Examples, the sound of a buzz saw whining shrilly outside the window during an intimate scene between the adulterous lovers in *The Touch,* and the moment when Ingrid Bergman shows her pathetic daughter just how a particular prelude should be played on the piano in *Autumn Sonata.* His misses are frequently more interesting than most people's scores. I'm thinking now of *From the Life of the Marionettes* and *After the Rehearsal.*

A digression here about style. The predominant arena for conflict in motion pictures has usually been the external, physical world. Certainly that was true for many years. Witness the staples of slapstick and Westerns, war films and chases and gangster movies and musicals. As the Freudian revolution sank in, however, the most fascinating arena of conflict shifted to the interior and films were faced with a problem. The psyche is not visible. If the most interesting fights are being waged in the heart and mind, what to do? Bergman evolved a style to deal with the human interior, and he alone among directors has explored the soul's battlefield to the fullest. With impunity he put his camera on faces for unconscionable periods of time while actors and actresses wrestled with their anguish. One saw great performers in extreme close-ups that lingered beyond where the textbooks say is good movie form. Faces were everything for him. Close-ups. More close-ups. Extreme close-ups. He created dreams and fantasies and so deftly mingled them with reality that gradually a sense of the human interior emerged. He used huge silences with tremendous effectiveness. The terrain of Bergman films is different from his contemporaries'. It matches the bleak beaches of the rocky island he lives on. He has found a way to show the soul's landscape. (He said he viewed the soul as a membrane, a red membrane, and showed it as such in *Cries and Whispers.*) By rejecting cinema's standard demand for conventional action, he has allowed wars to rage inside charac-

The peace of Stockholm's outer archipelago as filmed in Illicit Interlude *(1950), with Maj-Britt Nilsson*

ters that are as acutely visual as the movement of armies. See *Persona.*

All this, ladies and gentlemen, and he also works cheaply. He's fast; the films cost very little, and his tiny band of regulars can slap together a major work of art in half the time and for a tenth the price of what most take to mount some glitzy waste of celluloid. Plus he writes the scripts himself. What else could you ask for? Meaning, pro-

life story should be. There is no building saga of how he began and gradually worked himself up to dominate the Swedish stage and screen. The story skips around, back and forth, apparently depending on the author's spontaneity. It includes odd tales and feelings. An odd tale: as a young boy being locked inside a mortuary and becoming fascinated by the naked corpse of a young woman. A sad feeling: "My wife and I live near each other. One of us thinks and the other answers, or the other way round. I have no means of describing our affinity. One problem is insoluble. One day the blow will fall and separate us. No friendly god will turn us into a tree to shade the farm." It leaves out things you'd bet he'd discuss. His films, for instance. Well, maybe he doesn't leave them out exactly but there's much less than you'd expect, considering he's made over forty. There's also not much about his wives in this book. He's had plenty. (And lots of children too, though they're hardly mentioned.) That includes Liv Ullmann, who lived with him for years and was the mother of one of his children and a great star in his pictures. But there's not much about any of the actors and actresses in his films.

So what is there? Well, many gripping revelations, but they're mostly about his childhood. And about his theater work. Interestingly he draws a picture of every single scene before he stages it. And there is a moving account of how he directed Anders Ek, an actor in several films, who had developed leukemia and was using his own fear of approaching death to portray a Strindberg character. Bergman loves the theater. It's his real family. In fact, the warm, lovable family in *Fanny and Alexander* didn't exist for real — they were meant to symbolize the theater. (This isn't in the book. I happen to know it.) He writes too of his maladies: "I suffered from several indefinable illnesses and could never really decide whether I wanted to live at all." His weak body functions: "In all the theatres I have worked in for any length of time, I have been given my own lavatory."

His breakdown is in there too, over the income tax scandal. It's mesmerizing to read about

fundity, style, images, visual beauty, tension, storytelling flair, speed, economy, fecundity, innovation, an actor's director nonpareil. That's what I meant by the best, pound for pound. Perhaps other directors excel him in single areas, but nobody is as complete an artist in films.

O.K. — so now comes his book. It's a lot about stomach problems. But it's interesting. It's random, anecdotal. It's not chronological, as one's it. In 1976, Bergman was crudely snatched from a rehearsal and taken to police headquarters over money owed the Government because of his mishandling of income tax payments. It was not unlike the type of thing that occurs so frequently where one hires an accountant, presumes he will handle everything brilliantly and aboveboard, and finds later one has trustingly signed papers without understanding them or even reading them. The fact that he was innocent of willful dishonesty and a national treasure did not prevent the authorities from dealing with him harshly and boorishly. The result was a nervous breakdown, hospitalization, and self-imposed exile to Germany with profound feelings of rage and humiliation.

Finally, the picture one gets is of a highly emotional soul, not easily adaptable to life in this cold, cruel world, yet very professional and productive and, of course, a genius in the dramatic arts. In the translation by Joan Tate, Bergman writes quite well and one is often caught up and moved by his descriptions. I lapped up every page, but I'm no test because I have a great interest in this particular artist. It was hard for me to believe he has already turned seventy. In his book he recalls when at ten he was given a magic lantern, which projected shadows on the wall. It stimulated a love affair with movies that is touching in its depth of feeling. Now that he is world-renowned and retired from cinema, he writes the following: "My chair is comfortable, the room cosy, it grows dark and the first trembling picture is outlined on the white wall. It is quiet, the projector humming faintly in the well-insulated projection room. The shadows move, turning their faces towards me, urging me to pay attention to their destinies. Sixty years have gone by but the excitement is still the same."

ON INGMAR BERGMAN

FRANÇOIS TRUFFAUT

In addition to a brilliant film career, highlighted by such works as The 400 Blows, Shoot the Piano Player, *and* Jules and Jim, *François Truffaut was also known as an eminent film critic. He was a contributor to the famed French New Wave film journal* Cahiers du cinéma, *where these essays appeared, the first in 1958 and the second in 1973.*

Bergman's Opus

It's common knowledge that Ingmar Bergman, who is forty this year, is the son of a minister. Before he started to make films in 1945, he had written some plays and novels and was already deeply involved in directing a theater company — which he still is. He had mounted a broad range of plays by Anouilh, Camus, and masterpieces of French and Scandinavian classical literature.

This prodigious activity hasn't stopped him from making nineteen films in thirteen years, a fact all the more dizzying in that he usually creates them entirely, writing the screenplay as well as the dialogue, and directing them as well. Out of the nineteen, only six have been released commercially in France. *L'Eternel mirage* [*It Rains on Our Love*], *Summer with Monika, Smiles of a Summer Night, Sawdust and Tinsel* [*The Naked Night*], *The Seventh Seal,* and *Sommarlek* [*Illicit Interlude*]. But thanks to the prizes that Bergman has amassed during the past three years and to the fact that his films are finding a growing public in an increasing number of "art houses" (there are now eighteen in Paris), a number of his older films will open in first-run houses next season. I would

think that those most likely to find as wide an audience as, for example, *Smiles of a Summer Night* did are *A Lesson in Love* (a stunning comedy in the style of Lubitsch); *Waiting Women* [*Secrets of Women*], *Journey into Autumn* [*Dreams*], a comedy tinged with bitterness. Two other films, more ambitious, but uneven, might enjoy the kind of success that *Sawdust and Tinsel* had: *Prison* [*The Devil's Wanton*], the story of a film director whose old mathematics teacher has just proposed that he make a film about hell; and *Thirst* [*Three Strange Loves*], in which a couple of Swedish tourists traveling across war-torn Germany just after World War II become aware of their own double standards.

In Sweden, Ingmar Bergman is now considered the preeminent film director, but it wasn't by any means always that way. His first contact with cinema was in 1944 when he wrote the screenplay for *Torment* by Sjöberg (who also directed *Miss Julie*), the story of the "torments" that a Latin teacher named Caligula inflicts on his pupils. (Just before that, Bergman had mounted Camus's *Caligula*.) The next year he made his first film,

Crisis, about the woes of a young girl who is fought over by her natural mother and her adoptive mother. After that came *It Rains on Our Love* and *Port of Call,* among others.

Bergman's first films shocked audiences because of their pessimism and rebelliousness. They were almost always about a couple of adolescents searching for happiness in escapades at odds with middle-class society. These early movies were generally badly received. Bergman was treated like a subversive, blasphemous, and irritating schoolboy.

The first film that brought him real success was *Music in Darkness* [*Night Is My Future*] (released in 1948), the story of a pianist who goes blind during his military service. Once back in civilian life, he is patronized because of his infirmity until a rival in a love affair strikes him in anger. He goes mad with joy, simply because someone has finally treated him like a normal person. By 1951, Bergman had become fairly well recognized, but because of a crisis in the Swedish film industry no films were being made, and, in order to live, he made nine film commercials extolling the merits of a particular brand of soap.

The next year he went back to his real work with increased ardor, and made *Waiting Women,* which was probably influenced by Joseph Mankiewicz's *A Letter to Three Wives.*

Bergman's work is the labor of a born moviemaker. When he was six, he began to play with a tiny projector, using the same filmstrips over and over. In his film *Prison* he lingers lovingly over this childhood memory, showing us a movie buff who runs, in his attic, an old burlesque film in which a sleepwalker in a nightshirt, a policeman, and the devil himself chase each other in accelerated speed. Now, Bergman has a private film library of about 150 movies reduced to 16 millimeter that he often shows for his collaborators and actors.

Bergman has seen a lot of American films, and he appears to have been influenced by Hitchcock. One cannot help thinking of *Suspicion* and *Rich and Strange* when in *Thirst* one sees Bergman drawing out a dialogue between a man and a woman by the use of almost imperceptible but revealing gestures and the interplay of precise and rather stylized glances. Starting in 1948, the year Hitchcock's *The Rope* was released, Bergman stopped chopping up his footage and began to concentrate on moving his camera and his actors around more in order to construct longer uninterrupted episodes.

But unlike Juan Bardem, each of whose films is influenced by a different director and who has never succeeded in stamping his work with his own personality or sensibility, Bergman has perfectly incorporated in his own work the elements he admires in Cocteau, Anouilh, Hitchcock, and the classical theater.

Like Ophuls and Renoir, Bergman's work centers on women, but it evokes Ophuls more than it does Renoir, because the creator of *Sawdust and Tinsel,* like Ophuls, adopts the viewpoint of his female characters more spontaneously than that of his male characters. Specifically, one could say that Renoir beckons us to view his heroines through the eyes of their male partners, whereas Ophuls and Bergman tend to show us men through women's eyes. This is palpable in *Smiles of a Summer Night,* where the men are stock characters and the women are drawn with great subtlety.

A Swedish journal once noted that "Bergman is much wiser about women [than men]." Bergman replied, "All women move me — old, young, tall, short, fat, thin, thick, heavy, light, beautiful, charming, living, dead. I also love cows, she-monkeys, sows, bitches, mares, hens, geese, turkey hens, lady hippos, and mice. But the categories of female that I prefer are wild beasts and dangerous reptiles. There are women I loathe. I'd like to murder one or two, or have myself killed by one of them. The world of women is my universe. It's the world I have developed in, perhaps not for the best, but no man can really feel he knows himself if he manages to detach himself from it."

An increasing amount is written about Bergman and that's to the good. The critics who don't indulge in a tirade about the deep pessimism of

Lars Ekborg and Harriet Andersson embrace in Mon-ika *(1952)*

the Bergman opus usually go on about his optimism, both of which are true enough in terms of his overall work because he is a lover of truth. Bergman pushes stubbornly in all directions. This line of dialogue from *Smiles* sums up a philosophy of caring that is, nevertheless, tinged with Audiberti's mechanism: "What finally pushes us to the inaction of despair is that we cannot protect one single being from a single moment of suffering."

Bergman's early films pose social problems; in his second period the analysis becomes more personal, a purely introspective look into the hearts of his characters; and for the last few years, he has been preoccupied with good and evil and with metaphysics — which dominate *Sawdust and Tinsel* and *The Seventh Seal*. Thanks to the freedom allowed him by his Swedish producers

(practically all his films have been released by them in Scandinavia), Bergman has raced ahead, producing in thirteen years a cycle of creative work that took Hitchcock and Renoir thirty years.

There is a great deal of poetry in Bergman's work, but we become conscious of it after the fact. Rather, the essential elements are to be found in the search for a truth, which is always a more fruitful method. Bergman's preeminent strength is the direction he gives his actors. He entrusts the principal roles in his films to the five or six actors he loves best, never typecasting them. They are completely different from one film to the next, often playing diametrically opposite roles. He discovered Margit Carlqvist in a dress shop and Harriet Andersson, dressed in black tights, singing in a provincial revue. He rarely asks his actors to redo scenes, and he never changes a line of his dialogue, which he writes in one draft without any preestablished plan.

At the beginning of one of his films, the viewer has the feeling that Bergman himself doesn't yet know how he'll end his story and that may indeed sometimes be the case. With Renoir also one almost always has the impression of helping to shoot the film, of watching it as it becomes what it is going to be, of a kind of collaboration with the director.

It seems to me that the best proof of Bergman's success is that he impresses on us with such power characters born in his own imagination. So natural is the dialogue he gives them that it is both eloquent and, at the same time, sounds the way people talk. Bergman often cites O'Neill, concurring with him that "dramatic art that does not impinge on the relationship between man and God is without interest." This judgment perfectly describes *The Seventh Seal,* though I admit that I prefer *So Close to Life* [*Brink of Life*]. *The Seventh Seal* is an inquisitive meditation on death. *So Close to Life* is a meditative inquiry into birth. It amounts to the same thing; both are about life.

The action of *So Close* takes place in a maternity ward during a twenty-four-hour period. I can't improve on the description of the story and the meaning of the film given by Ulla Isaksson, who wrote it with Bergman.

Life, birth, death are secrets — secrets for which some are called to live, while others are condemned to die.

We can assail both the heavens and the sciences with questions — there is only one answer. Wherever life is lived, the living are rewarded with both anguish and happiness.

The woman who thirsts for tenderness is deceived by her desires and must accept her sterility. The woman who is bursting with life is not allowed to keep the child she waited for so passionately. The young woman, so inexperienced in life, is suddenly surprised by it when she is thrown into a crowd of women in childbirth.

Life touches them all — without posing questions or offering answers — it goes on its way without interruption toward new births, new lives. Only human beings ask questions.

In contrast to *The Seventh Seal,* which is inspired by medieval stained-glass windows and filled with tableaux, *So Close* was shot with the utmost simplicity. The background is always secondary to the three heroines, and, by the same token, Bergman intrudes as little as possible on Ulla Isaksson's story. Eva Dahlbeck, Ingrid Thulin, and above all Bibi Andersson are remarkably accurate and feeling in their portrayals. There is no musical accompaniment; everything is geared to a purity of line. What is most striking in Bergman's latest films is their lack of frills. Anyone born into this world and living in it can understand and appreciate them. I think Bergman reaches an enormous audience around the world because he speaks with such astounding simplicity.

Cries and Whispers

It begins like Chekhov's *Three Sisters* and ends like *The Cherry Orchard* and in between it's more like Strindberg. *Cries and Whispers,* Ingmar Bergman's latest film, was a tremendous success in London and New York, and the sensation of the Cannes Festival last week. It will open in Paris in September. Unanimously considered a masterpiece, *Cries and Whispers* is going to bring back to Bergman the public that has been avoiding him since his last great success, *The Silence,* was released in 1963.

Yet there has been no body of work of the caliber and integrity of Bergman's since the war. Between 1945 and 1972 he made thirty-three movies. His name became well known with the success in Cannes in 1956 of *Smiles of a Summer Night,* his sixteenth film. Ten years earlier the first

Monika's disillusionment after the summer's dream in Monika *(1952)*

Bergman film to be shown in France had been noticed by only one critic, André Bazin, who congratulated the young Swedish director for "creating a world of blinding cinematic purity" (review of *L'Eternel mirage* in *L'Ecran Français,* September 1947).

Since 1957, almost all of Bergman's films have eventually come out in France, though not in the right order. The most famous are *Sawdust and Tinsel, The Seventh Seal, Wild Strawberries, The Virgin Spring, The Silence,* and *Persona;* the most touching are *Sommarlek, Summer with Monika, Les Communicants* [*Winter Light*], *The Rite* [*The Ritual*]. Let's speak briefly about *The Rite.*

For the past few weeks, this extraordinary film, shot by Bergman in black and white for Swedish television, has been playing in Paris. The theater of the Studio Galande is tiny, and the eighty spectators who come each day to see it don't cover the costs of showing it. In a move of real stupidity, *The Rite* was closed the day before Bergman arrived in Cannes; his arrival was an event we've been hoping for for fifteen years. Taking *The Rite* off the bill last week is like taking an author's book out of the bookstore window the day he receives the Prix Goncourt. What a mess! And a mess for which the Paris critics have to bear some responsibility. A film of extreme inner violence, *The Rite* shows us three artists executing a judge — in other words, a critic. It is curious, then, that the press chose to ignore this film.

Bergman is a stubborn, shy man. He devotes his whole life to the theater and movies, and one has the sense that he is only happy when he's working surrounded by actresses, and that in the near future one won't see a Bergman film without women. I think he's more involved in the feminine principle than in feminism. Women are not seen through a masculine prism in his films, but are observed in a spirit of total complicity. His female characters are infinitely subtle, while his male characters are conventions.

Instead of squeezing four hours' worth of material into an hour and a half, as most contemporary directors do, Bergman works with short stories — a few characters, very little action, little in the way of stage effects, a brief time frame. Each of his films — it's fascinating to see them together in a week-long retrospective or at a festival — reminds us of a single painting in an exposition. There are Bergman "periods." The present period is more physical than metaphysical. The strange title *Cries and Whispers* stays with you as you come away from watching the film, having been cried to and whispered to.

Bergman's lesson is threefold: freedom of dialogue, radical cleanness of the image, and absolute priority of the human face.

As far as freedom of dialogue goes, the text of his films is not meant to be a piece of literature, but simple spoken words — actually spoken and unspoken words — confessions and confidences. We could also have learned this lesson from Jean Renoir, but curiously it comes through with greater weight by means of a foreign and cinematically virginal language. This has been evident since *Sommarlek* — the film of our salad days, of our twenties, of our first loves. As we watch a Bergman film, our senses are strongly involved. Our ears hear Swedish — it's like a piece of music or a dark color — and we read the subtitles, which simplify and reinforce the dialogue. If you are interested enough to compare Buñuel's Mexican or Spanish films with the ones he made in France, you can reflect on this phenomenon of shifted communication.

Consider the cleanness of his images. Some filmmakers allow pure chance to enter into their images — the sun, passersby, a bicycle (filmmakers like Rossellini, Lelouch, and Huston) and others want to control every square inch of the screen (Eisenstein, Lang, and Hitchcock). Bergman started out like the first group and then changed camps. In his latest films you never see a chance pedestrian; your attention will never be distracted by an extra object in the setting, even a bird in the garden. There is nothing on the canvas except what Bergman (who's antipictorial, like all true filmmakers) wants there.

The human face. No one draws so close to it as Bergman does. In his recent films there is nothing more than mouths talking, ears listening, eyes expressing curiosity, hunger, panic.

Listen to the words of love that Max von Sydow addresses to Liv Ullmann in *Hour of the Wolf,* filmed in 1966. Then listen to the hate-filled words the same couple hurl at each other in *The Passion of Anna,* filmed two years later. What you hear is the most mercilessly autobiographical director working in movies today.

His most rueful film is *Now About These Women* [*All These Women*]. It's ironic to realize that Bergman's finest work is precisely involved in bringing out the dormant genius in each of the actresses he's chosen to work with — Maj-Britt Nilsson, Harriet Andersson, Eva Dahlbeck, Gunnel Lindblom, Ingrid Thulin, Bibi Andersson, Liv Ullmann. They are not kittens or dolls but real women. Bergman films them as they look out at the world, their gazes increasingly intense with toughness and suffering. The results are wonderful movies that, like Renoir's, are as simple as saying hello. However, is saying hello so very simple?

Translated by Leonard Mayhew

Bergmanorama

JEAN-LUC GODARD

One of the "New Wave" film directors of the sixties and seventies, Jean-Luc Godard also contributed many articles to Cahiers du cinéma, *including this one, published in 1958. Among his landmark films for the French New Wave are* Breathless, Alphaville, *and* Weekend.

THERE ARE FIVE OR SIX FILMS IN CINEMATIC HISTORY ONE would like to review with these words alone: "This is the most beautiful of films!" For there is no higher praise. Films like Murnau/Flaherty's *Taboo,* Rossellini's *A Voyage to Italy,* and Claude Renoir's *The Golden Coach* require no lengthy discourses. Like starfish opening and closing, they know how to open, then conceal the secrets of a world they alone possess and at the same time fascinatingly reflect. Theirs is the only truth. It is deeply imbedded in them, even though it is constantly exposed to the world on the silver screen.

"This is the most beautiful of films!" says it all. Why? It just *is* so. Only the cinema can express itself with such childish simplicity, without false modesty. Why? Because it is the cinema. And the cinema is self-sufficient. To praise the merits of Wells, Ophuls, Dreyer, Hawks, Cukor, and even Vadim, it suffices to say: This is cinema! We could also say the same in comparing them with the great artists of centuries past.

On the contrary, it is hard to imagine a critic praising Faulkner's latest novel by saying, "This is literature," or saying of Stravinsky or Paul Klee,

"This is music" or "This is painting." It would be even more unthinkable to refer in this way to Shakespeare, Mozart, or Raphael. Among book publishers, it would not occur to the likes of Bernard Grasset to launch a poet with a slogan like "This is poetry!" Even Jean Vilar would blush if he wrote on a poster for Le Cid "This is theater!"

But "This is film!" is not only a catchword but also a battle cry to both marketers and filmmakers. In short, one of the seldom-discussed privileges when it comes to film is that it can justify its existence merely by existing, thereby basing its aesthetics on its ethics. Five or six films, I said, plus one, because *Illicit Interlude* is the most beautiful of films.

Great artists are probably distinguished by the fact that you can barely utter their name before it becomes impossible otherwise to explain the many sensations and feelings that overwhelm you under certain exceptional circumstances, confronted by a wondrous scene of an unexpected event: Beethoven under the stars, upon a cliff with waves crashing against it; Balzac, when looking down from Montmartre so that it seems

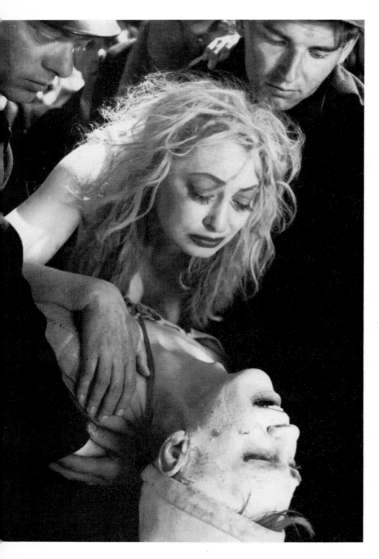

Anders Ek as the white circus clown (Frost) and Gudrun Brost as his wife (Alma) in The Naked Night *(1953)*

as if all of Paris is at your feet. So if the present and the past play hide-and-seek in the face of your beloved; if death urges you with icy irony to try to live on when, humiliated and hurt, you ask the supreme question; if the words "sweet summer," "last vacation," "eternal mirage," reach your lips, then, without thinking about it, you have named the man whom the French ciné-mathèque has confirmed — through a second retrospective for those who have seen only a few of his nineteen films — as the most original filmmaker in Europe: Ingmar Bergman.

Original? *The Seventh Seal* and *The Naked Night* fit this description; so does *Smiles of a Summer Night*. But *Monika, Dreams,* and *To Joy* could be relatives of Maupassant. As for technique, the camera angles are already there in Germaine Dulac, the effects in Man Ray, the reflections on the water in Kirsanoff, and the flashbacks can be regarded more or less as banished nowadays. Is it passé? No, the cinema is different, the advocates of technique exclaim; above all, it is a profession.

Not at all! Film is no profession. It is an art. It is not teamwork. One is always alone, both in the studio and in front of the empty page. And for Bergman, to be alone is to ask questions. And to make films is to answer them. One could not come closer to the classical definition of romanticism.

He is, of course, the only one of our contemporary filmmakers who does not openly repudiate the working methods embraced by the avant gardistes of the 1930s, which pop up even today at every experimental or amateur film festival.

But in the case of the film *Three Strange Loves,* these methods should instead be regarded as a bold move by its director. Because Bergman used this mishmash with completely different films in mind. In Bergman's aesthetics, those scenes of lakes, forests, grass, and clouds, seemingly original camera angles and overly artful backlighting are not an abstract demonstration of the cameraman's prowess. Instead they reflect the psyche of his characters at a *particular moment,* when Bergman wishes to express an equally particular feeling, for example Monika's elation when she takes a boat through Stockholm at dawn and her dejection when she returns the same way through a sleeping city.

At a particular moment. Ingmar Bergman is the filmmaker of particular moments. His films are shaped from the main character's reflections about the present and are made more profound by splitting up time — in the manner of Proust but much more powerfully, as if Proust were multiplied by both Joyce and Rousseau all at once, resulting in a gigantic and enormous *meditation based on one moment.* A Bergman film is, so to speak, a twenty-fourth of a second transformed and extended to an hour and a half. It is the world compressed between two blinks of the eye, the sadness between two beats of the heart, the joy of living between two claps of the hands.

Thus the primordial importance of flashbacks in these solitary walks through Scandinavian dream landscapes. In *Illicit Interlude,* Maj-Britt Nilsson need only cast a glance at herself in the mirror in order to take off like an Orpheus or Lancelot in pursuit of paradise lost and time rediscovered. Used almost systematically by Bergman in most of his works, flashbacks thus cease to be the "poor tricks" Orson Welles referred to. They become, if not the actual subject of a film, at least its absolute prerequisite.

This stylistic technique has, moreover, the incomparable advantage of giving substance to the script by supplying both its internal rhythm and its dramatic core. Look at any Bergman film at all and you will notice that every flashback always begins or ends in the proper place, or, rather, in two places. His skill lies in the fact that the change of scene, exactly as in Hitchcock's best works, is always connected to the main character's feelings. In other words, it propels the plot forward, which is the mark of a great filmmaker. What we take as something easy is actually a source of great stringency. The autodidactic Ingmar Bergman, as some "professional" filmmakers

derisively call him, has something to teach the best of our scriptwriters in this respect. As we will see, this is not the first time.

When Vadim made his breakthrough, we applauded him as the man of the hour, while most of his colleagues were far behind. When we saw the poetic mimicry of Giulietta Masina, we likewise applauded Fellini for his baroque freshness, which felt like springtime. But this renaissance of the modern cinema had already reached its peak five years earlier, thanks to the son of a Swedish pastor.

What were we dreaming about when *Monika* showed up on the movie screens of Paris? Everything we blamed our French filmmakers for not doing, Ingmar Bergman had already done. *Monika* was a forerunner of *And God Created Woman,* but done perfectly. And the final scene of *Nights of Cabiria,* with Giulietta Masina staring blindly into the camera: have we forgotten that it was right there in the next-to-last scene of *Monika?*

The sudden conspiracy between viewer and actor that André Bazin is so fond of: we forgot that we had seen it done a thousand times more powerfully and poetically by Harriet Andersson in the scene where she looked straight into the camera with laughing but confused eyes and let us witness her chagrin in choosing hell instead of heaven.

All that glitters is not gold. All those who cry from the rooftops are not innovators. A truly original auteur never creates for his own society. Bergman shows us that innovation is precision, and precision is profundity. What is profoundly new about *Illicit Interlude, Monika, Three Strange Loves,* and *The Seventh Seal* is above all their admirably precise tone. Bergman calls a spade a spade. But so do others, and this is of minor importance. The important thing is that, endowed with an unfailing moral elegance, Bergman is able to deal with any truth, including the most indelicate (cf. the final scene of *Secrets of Women*).

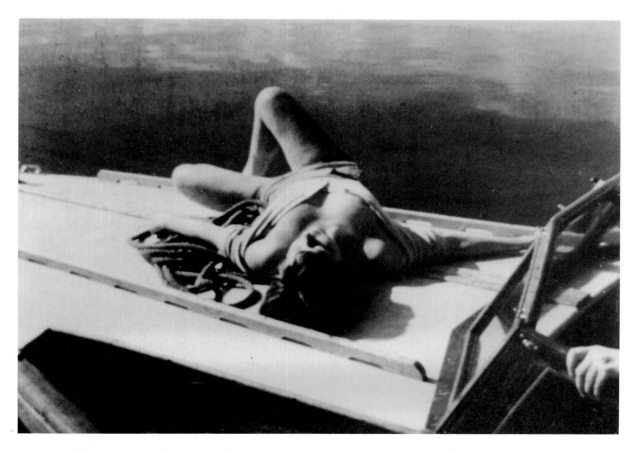

Harriet Andersson as Monika in Monika *(1952)*

What is profound is his unpredictability, and every new film by this auteur surprises even his most enthusiastic supporters. If you expect a comedy, it ends up being a medieval mystery tale. The only thing his films usually have in common is Bergman's incredible ease in portraying situations, where he even beats Feydeau; the credibility of his dialogue, which surpasses Montherlant's; and his modesty, which paradoxically leaves Giraudoux behind. It goes without saying that in addition to this supreme ease in working out his scripts, while the camera is humming Bergman possesses an absolute mastery in directing the actors. In this domain, Ingmar Bergman is the equal of Cukor or Renoir.

It is worth mentioning that most of his play-ers, many of whom belong to his theater ensemble, are outstanding at their craft. I am thinking especially of Maj-Britt Nilsson, whose obstinate chin and scornful pout are reminiscent of Ingrid Bergman. But having seen Birger Malmsten as a dreamy youth in *Illicit Interlude* and then as the unrecognizable sleek-haired bourgeois in *Three Strange Loves,* Gunnar Björnstrand and Harriet Andersson in the first episode of *Dreams* and then with entirely different looks, new tics, and different body rhythms in *Smiles of a Summer Night,* one realizes Bergman's prodigious talent in shaping his "cattle," as Hitchcock called them.

Is it so certain that script conflicts with direction? Alex Joffé and René Clément, for instance, are entirely comparable in terms of talent. But when talent borders on genius, as in *Illicit Interlude* and Visconti's *White Nights,* is it not a waste of time to discuss endlessly who is superior to the other, the complete auteur or the pure director? Perhaps not, because one is talking about two different approaches to the cinema, one of which may be superior to the other.

There are, essentially, two kinds of filmmakers. Those who walk along the street with their eyes on the ground and those who walk with their heads high. Those in the first category have to look up in order to see what is going on around them, letting their eyes sweep from left to right and gathering a series of images of what is before them. They *see.* The others see nothing; they *look,* fixing their attention on the particular point that interests them. When they make films, those in the first category produce images that are airy and fluid (Rossellini), those in the second category produce millimeter-exact images (Hitchcock). Among the first category, one will undoubtedly find images that are very disparate but terribly sensitive to the accidents of the moment (Welles); among the second, extremely precise camera movements which have their own abstract value in space (Lang). Bergman belongs to the first category, the free filmmakers. Visconti belongs to the second, the rigorous filmmakers.

As for myself, I prefer *Monika* to *Senso* and the auteur approach to that of the director. Except for Renoir, Bergman is clearly the most prominent representative of this approach in Europe. If *The Devil's Wanton* is not sufficient proof of this, it is at least an obvious symbol. The theme is familiar: a director is offered a manuscript about the devil from his mathematics teacher. But he is not the one who falls victim to all the diabolic misadventures. Instead it is the scriptwriter whom he asks to polish the story.

As a man of the theater, Bergman is willing to direct other people's plays. But as a filmmaker he wants to be the master of all he surveys. Unlike Bresson or Visconti, who reshape things that are rarely personal to them, Bergman creates his stories and characters *ex nihilo.* Nobody can deny that *The Seventh Seal* is less skillfully directed than *White Nights,* its images are less precise, its camera angles less rigorous. But — and herein lies the great distinction — for such an immense talent as Visconti's it suffices to rely on his good taste to make a good film. He knows what he is doing and, in a certain sense, he makes it easy for himself. If a person knows he has such a gift, it is not difficult to select beautiful curtains, perfect furniture, and the only correct camera movements. An artist who is too conscious of himself is often tempted to choose the easiest path.

What is difficult, in contrast, is to move ahead onto unknown ground, discover dangers, take risks, be afraid. The scene in *White Nights* with the snowflakes falling around the boat carrying Maria Schell and Marcello Mastroianni is sublime. But this sublime scene is nothing compared to the one in *To Joy* where the old orchestra conductor is lying stretched out on the grass, watching Stig Olin cast loving glances at Maj-Britt Nilsson on her lounge chair, and thinking "How does one depict a scene of such great beauty?" I admire *White Nights,* but I love *Illicit Interlude.*

Translated by Victor Kayfetz

PART THREE

ACTORS ON BERGMAN

Working with Bergman: Excerpts from a Seminar with Liv Ullmann

Liv Ullmann first achieved international recognition as a film actress through her work with Ingmar Bergman in such films as Persona, Autumn Sonata, The Passion of Anna, *and* Cries and Whispers. *In addition to her stage and screen acting career, she is a best-selling author and, most recently, a film director. This seminar, sponsored by the American Film Institute, occurred in 1973.*

INTRODUCTION: Let's start off with an obvious question: How does Ingmar Bergman work with and direct his actors?

LIV ULLMANN: He is very different from what most people believe. He has a reputation of a demon, which is totally untrue. He depends very much on his actors. He knows whom he has hired. He listens to them and he watches them. He tries to get out of them what they have to give, not what he would want to do in a similar situation. He is a fantastic listener and he has a fantastic manner of looking. He sees what you are trying to express and he builds on that. He helps get it out of you. He also makes very good scenery. Do you call it scenery? I mean the movements of the scene are always telling in itself, very much of the scene. He doesn't explain very much.

QUESTION: Do you mean his blocking of the scene?

ULLMANN: Yes, his blocking of the scene, in that blocking actually is what he wants the scene to be like, and then it is up to the actor to film it.

QUESTION: Where does he actually sit?

ULLMANN: He sits very close to the camera. You feel him very much and if he is not close to the camera, you tend to act toward him. He always is very, very close to the camera and he is terribly inspiring. I don't know what his magic is, but it is something that makes you want to give everything you have.

QUESTION: Does he tell you that or is it something you have to feel out?

ULLMANN: He hates to discuss and analyze. He believes that if you have chosen your profession as an actor, then you know a little how to act. He assumes that you are fairly intelligent. He feels that an analysis would take away the fantasy. He knows that is the way an actor creates. The actor has to use his own fantasy and imagination.

QUESTION: How many takes does Bergman usually shoot of a scene?

ULLMANN: It depends. Sometimes he uses the first take. Sometimes we go on for 20, 30, or 40 takes until you are completely exhausted.

QUESTION: Does he allow rehearsals?

ULLMANN: Yes, he allows technical rehearsals. He

likes to take on the first emotional rehearsal because sometimes that is the best take.

QUESTION: I am interested in a scene in *Persona* where Bibi Andersson sits down and tells you the story about your marriage and your boy. Could you take that as an example?

ULLMANN: That was very strange because he did that with two cameras. There was one on Bibi when she told my story and there was one camera on me while she was telling the story. It was supposed to be cut up, using the best from each. But when he saw it as a whole, he didn't know what to pick. So he used them both. Many people have tried to analyze why he does this. The real reason is that both told something there which he felt was important. He couldn't choose which one was most important so he had both.

QUESTION: What does one of his [Bergman's] scripts look like?

ULLMANN: The last picture I did for him is *Cries and Whispers,* with Harriet Andersson, Ingrid Thulin, and me. That was more like a personal letter. It starts, "My Dear Friends: We're now going to make a film together. It is sort of a vision that I have and I will try to describe it." He describes it in fifty pages. That was his script.

QUESTION: You got the script before the shooting started?

ULLMANN: Yes. It was like taking off from there. He did all of it in natural light. We had no artificial light. We filmed everything in a big castle. He used big windows. From sunrise until sundown, he used the natural light in its stages. I think it will be exceptional.

QUESTION: Was it shot in the winter or during the summer?

ULLMANN: It was shot during the autumn. He made the movie for his own company. He said, "[If] I am not happy with it, I won't release it, but it is an experience for me. It is my own workmanship. Because it is our film, if we are all happy with it, then we will release it."

QUESTION: That is why all the actors with leading roles were also listed as being producers?

ULLMANN: Being producers meant that he didn't have to pay us. As for us actors, we thought that being producers we would have a say in the production. But that wasn't so. What it all amounted to was that he didn't pay us.

QUESTION: Does that mean that you don't have as much say as you would like when you work with Bergman?

ULLMANN: I have a say as an actress. As I said, he respects everybody who works with him and that includes his actors. In this film, however, we thought that we would have something to say about publicity and our working hours. But all these decisions remained his. It was his picture.

QUESTION: How much improvisation is there in a Bergman film?

ULLMANN: More and more. In my experience it started in *Shame.* If you remember, they are sitting at a table drinking wine and eating. Then they fall down on the grass. That was improvised. We knew what he wanted. But it was more or less up to us.

QUESTION: That was a change from the way he had directed you before?

ULLMANN: Yes. He has always been very strict in wanting us to keep to his sentences. There was the dinner party in *The Passion of Anna* where the four tell their own story. In that scene, we had complete freedom. But we had to stick to the character. One day a lady arrived and made a beautiful dinner. Max von Sydow drank red wine and all of us asked him questions. He had to answer as the character and the camera was on him all the time. Bergman did the same thing with all four of us. Then he edited it.

QUESTION: There are scenes in *The Passion of Anna* where he interviews each of the actors. Did he write those interviews?

ULLMANN: No. As it was before, in the script he had written what the characters themselves spoke as characters. Then he had written a text. Do you understand what I mean? He broke the picture in four places. The characters sort of came out and spoke as the character.

Liv Ullmann and Max von Sydow in Shame *(1967)*

QUESTION: Yes, but you speak as an actor.

ULLMANN: Yes, because then he didn't really feel that it was good. He took it away, and after the picture was finished he asked us to come to the studio and to speak as actors. Bibi Andersson used the text from her character.

QUESTION: You have played different women's roles in Bergman's films. How accurate do you think his interpretations of the different women have been?

ULLMANN: They are accurate for that sort of woman. I think he has a great understanding for women, maybe even more than for men. I think his women characters, especially in the last years, have been more interesting.

QUESTION: Does he allow you to tell him more about what you would feel if you were that woman?

ULLMANN: First of all, he knows which actor is going to play which part when he writes the script. So he knows something of what he is going to get. He is also very open for suggestions. He hates it if you start to analyze, but he is very open to your own kind of interpretation of the kind of woman that he has written.

QUESTION: Besides acting, have you thought of other things that you would like to do with film? Would you like to do photography or directing?

ULLMANN: No. I would like to write, but not for film.

QUESTION: Earlier you were talking about Bergman putting a lot of himself into his women characters.

ULLMANN: Yes. I think there is very much of himself in both the men and the women. People tend to believe that his pictures are from his own private life, what he's like just in that moment. I don't believe that is true. Of course, he uses his own experience but in a different way. I think he uses his experience of life and people. I don't recognize any real situation or real human being. You suggested that in *The Passion of Anna* I was maybe a part of Anna. There might be parts of you which he puts into the character that he wants you to play but I never killed my first husband. It is very difficult for us when people think that.

QUESTION: There is a kind of ensemble company about Bergman. How much do the actors feed into him in the preparation of the script? I am speaking of anything they do aside from improvisation and for the camera.

ULLMANN: Nothing. We have nothing to do with the script. He is writing a script now which we are going to shoot in the fall. He just asks you, "Do you want to be in my next picture?"

QUESTION: He doesn't show you the script at all?

ULLMANN: Not before it is finished. Of course, you can suddenly say, "No," but I don't think that has happened.

QUESTION: On *Cries and Whispers,* was the letter that you received beforehand the only preparation for the film?

ULLMANN: But there were actually fifty pages, and we used the letter in the filming. He described his visions.

QUESTION: Did everybody get the same letter?

ULLMANN: Yes.

QUESTION: Then it was all improvised?

ULLMANN: Yes. But it was very clear. He said, "I see a room, a red room. There are three women dressed in white and they are moving slowly about." That is a scene. From there on he made the blocking.

QUESTION: But the dialogue wasn't in the letter?

ULLMANN: Very little. He said, "I feel that they are talking about love and about being afraid." But the dialogue was not blocked out.

QUESTION: You people all know each other as you have been working together for a long time. How much of the real feelings that you have about each other are used by him in terms of realities in the scene? Does he make use of your own personal feelings about each other?

ULLMANN: No. I don't think so.

QUESTION: He just goes for the imaginary situation?

ULLMANN: Yes.

QUESTION: He does not get results from real relationships outside?

ULLMANN: Bibi Andersson and I are close friends, but except in *Persona* we have not worked closely together. The same is true with Max von Sydow. Ingrid Thulin and I have no relationship with each other.

QUESTION: So it's primarily the imaginary situation that you work on?

ULLMANN: Yes, absolutely.

QUESTION: What happens to you when you are making a film? Are you living together, like on the island?

ULLMANN: We are forced to. In the summer this island has a big sand shore.

QUESTION: Beach?

ULLMANN: Yes, a beach. There are a lot of tourists there. Usually when he has made pictures there, he has rented all the small tourist houses. Each crew member has a little tourist house. They bring their families. It's not that we live together. We all have individual lives apart from the set.

QUESTION: On pictures like *Persona,* how many weeks before the shooting started did you get the script? Also how long did you rehearse before shooting?

ULLMANN: We did not rehearse at all. We got the script, actually, because he had been very sick. They did not know if they were going to make the picture at all. They just asked Bibi Andersson and me to be free for the summer and they would pay us something if the picture didn't come off. He finished the script and it was decided very shortly before, three weeks before, that they would make the picture. We had one meeting at Bibi Andersson's house where he told us some of his visions about the script. That was all done before we started. To me it was very difficult because I didn't know him before. I was terribly shy and frightened because he was sort of a god to me.

QUESTION: So, in fact, you rehearsed with the technical crew before the shooting started. Was it just before he shot?

ULLMANN: Just before each shot. He never has rehearsals before the actual shooting starts.

QUESTION: That scene in which you created a great mood where you were humming as you went out in the country, was that the first take? You were peeling mushrooms and humming.

ULLMANN: He got the idea of that actual situation when we were sitting in between takes with our big hats. We were humming. He said, "This is wonderful. It looks relaxed. I want this in the picture." That was perhaps the only time when he used a personal relationship.

QUESTION: The scene where he uses the two cameras, how long did you rehearse before the first take?

ULLMANN: Not very much. It was a very long dialogue for Bibi Andersson. He doesn't believe in rehearsing long dialogues.

QUESTION: Were you surprised to see the ending of the film?

ULLMANN: Of *Persona?* Yes, very much. Much of that picture happened at the cutting table. This scene was not in the script. Also the scene where the two faces come together, we did not know about that either. He took us once to the cutting room. We hadn't heard about this. He said, "I want you to watch something." We saw the strange face. I thought, "Oh, God, Bibi is fantastic. She looks completely neurotic." At the same time, Bibi thought, "How did Liv do it?" Suddenly we saw that it was half of each. It

was really frightening. That was an idea he had thought about during the shooting.

QUESTION: Were the effects, the picture of the film breaking, and the excerpt from the early Swedish comedy in the script?

ULLMANN: No.

QUESTION: He put them in later?

ULLMANN: Yes. It might have been in his special script, however. But it was not in ours.

QUESTION: His special script?

ULLMANN: Yes, he sometimes does that.

QUESTION: What is his special script?

ULLMANN: It is more or less a technical script between him and Sven Nykvist, his photographer.

QUESTION: What kind of dialogue does he carry on with Nykvist?

ULLMANN: Not very much. They have worked together for a long time. Sven Nykvist is not verbal at all. They sort of feel each other. The way friends work when they know each other very well. You don't have to speak very much.

QUESTION: When does Bergman bring Nykvist into a production? Will he show him the script earlier than the actors?

ULLMANN: Not that I know of. I think we all get it at the same time. They prepare together. They experiment a lot with colors and lights. On this last picture with the natural light from the windows, they lived in this castle for three weeks and experimented. They woke up very early in the morning and took pictures.

QUESTION: This was before the shooting started?

ULLMANN: Yes.

QUESTION: Do you look at your own dailies?

ULLMANN: Not with him. He says that he doesn't mind but I think that he would mind. Also, I trust him. If I am working with a director that I am not sure of, then I like to look at them. But mostly it is better not to do it.

QUESTION: How did you prepare for the role in *Persona* where you didn't have dialogue to either play with or against?

Bergman directing Liv Ullmann as Eva on the set of
Autumn Sonata *(1977)*

ULLMANN: I had to read the script many times. It was very difficult for me because I was twenty-four at the time. I had experienced a lot which I didn't know about then. The way that I prepared was to read the script many times, to try to block it into sections. I tried to think, "This is the section where this is happening to her, and now he goes a little further with this section." I very often work this way. I divide the manuscript into sections. It always helps you know where you are at the shooting.

QUESTION: Perhaps we can talk about some specific scenes and what you tried to present within the context of a certain scene. For instance, there is a dialogue in *Shame* where you and Max von Sydow are drinking a bottle of wine and are having a conversation about having a child. What specifically within the context of the character did you go for and how did you go for it?

ULLMANN: To me it was the last time when these people were happy. It was the last time when they had a sort of hope in their lives. What was important for me to express in that scene was love for him. Whatever the character said and did there was done primarily to express that. If you didn't know this about her, I feel that the tragedy that these people would never have hope again in life wouldn't be so big. You needed to know that they had love and happiness and hope in them at one time.

QUESTION: There was an interesting intoxication

about the scene. How did you approach the particular feeling in this scene?

ULLMANN: I don't know. Sometimes it is a help when a scene says that you are in a specific mood. But that takes you away from the way you would have reacted in that particular situation. You have a little background if you know that "here I am a little drunk" or "here I am a little afraid." Even if this isn't supposed to show too much, all the time it is in the background and it helps you act out the scene.

QUESTION: Have you worked in very many stage productions and in any directed by Bergman?

ULLMANN: Yes. I worked six years in Norway. I am Norwegian so I wanted to work on the stage in Norway. I worked with Bergman in *Peer Gynt*.

QUESTION: His directing must be very different.

ULLMANN: Yes, it is. There he speaks much more. He really speaks. He is fantastic. You should meet him. He is a verbal genius. The actors in Norway just adore him. The biggest actors will take small parts just to work with him. I learned more from that stage play than I ever learned anywhere.

QUESTION: You seem to be a very sensitive person. I was wondering if, in the ensemble with Bergman, everybody is pretty much that way?

ULLMANN: Yes, maybe.

QUESTION: What kind of a relationship do you have with Sven Nykvist, as well as with the rest of the ensemble?

ULLMANN: We are very good friends. We have worked together on so many pictures, also apart from Ingmar. Sven Nykvist is very timid and shy.

QUESTION: Is he also sensitive?

ULLMANN: Yes, he is very sensitive, but he never comes out with it. He is a perfectionist. On one picture he and Ingmar were looking at the daily rushes and he had done something wrong with the light. Ingmar had said that he should not have used one of the lights but Nykvist used it. When they saw the rushes Ingmar was very

angry, because they had to shoot it once more. Ingmar told Nykvist that he was an idiot. Nykvist was so timid that he didn't say a word.

QUESTION: I thought that *Shame* was one of the finest antiwar films ever made.

ULLMANN: Yes. I thought that I was doing something very important.

QUESTION: Bergman and the other actors felt that way too?

ULLMANN: Yes. I think that everybody felt a part of it. I am very sorry that in Sweden they were very much against the picture, especially the left wing. They felt that he didn't take sides. That is what the picture was all about. You can't take sides.

QUESTION: Which Bergman film did you enjoy working in the most? Do you have a preference?

ULLMANN: I think *Shame* meant the most to me. *Cries and Whispers* I also thought was very good.

QUESTION: Do you see the films in which you don't act?

ULLMANN: I have seen all of them.

QUESTION: Did you see *The Touch?*

ULLMANN: Yes.

QUESTION: Did you talk to Bergman about what you thought of it?

ULLMANN: Yes.

QUESTION: Is there a certain charisma about Bergman within the ensemble of actors? Do they put him on a certain level because of the aura about him, even though they know him very well?

ULLMANN: Yes. There is something about him. This is not always in private. In private he is very amusing. But on the set, there is something about him. A magic. Especially when he is sitting behind the camera. You feel that you are a part of something special. I can't really explain it very well. But he has an aura about him. It's his eyes and his ears.

QUESTION: Are you nervous when you work with

him? Are you always trying to outdo yourself?

ULLMANN: No, I feel relaxed. I know that he will help and he will know what I am trying to express. If I don't do it, then I know that he will help me. He will never say that I am phony or bad. He has respect for actors and for everybody. A bad director very often doesn't have that respect.

THE BERGMAN VACCINATION METHOD

ERLAND JOSEPHSON

A writer and actor, Erland Josephson has worked with Ingmar Bergman in many capacities for almost half a century. They have coauthored screenplays together, and Bergman has directed Josephson in many productions for stage, screen, and television, including Scenes from a Marriage *and* Fanny and Alexander. *A long-time member, and former head, of the Royal Dramatic Theater, Josephson played the title role in Bergman's 1994 production of* The Goldberg Variations *there.*

By all appearances, Ingmar Bergman is a successful man. But those who study his autobiography and have perchance never heard his name must think they are reading about a man of almost endless shortcomings, an unusually intriguing failure both in the arts and in his life during the twentieth century in a faraway country called Sweden.

The fact that *The Magic Lantern* reads like this is not an expression of coquetry, but part of Bergman's strategy for dealing with life. If the last generation of his contemporaries or posterity should reassess him, then so what? He was the first one to the punch and is consequently not the least bit surprised. He has, moreover, consigned himself to oblivion in an unforgettable way. This is a clever technique for not letting himself be obliterated.

A man obsessed with failure has succeeded better than others in portraying it.

This could be referred to as the Bergman vaccination method. The only thing that can prevent a poison from spreading is that poison itself. The only way to face demons is to conjure them

up. And the more chaotic your feelings, the stricter order you impose. Such order not only pervades Bergman's theatrical set design and cinematic camera angles, but also takes charge of all the movements, angles, and details of his everyday life. Everything must be predictable and predicted. The only thing allowed to surprise Bergman and others is Bergman himself. He wants to know where everyone stands: colleagues, friends, obstructionists, enemies. But no one should know where he stands. Freedom can be found only in lack of freedom. Not to be surprised by people requires getting to know them. Bergman approaches the great works with matchless intuition and insight. He is a brilliant reader. Then he folds the living into the pattern of the fictional. The stage is the platform of truth.

He sketches his own patterns of truth into his films. Art is a matter of letting everything happen before it happens.

Thus he practices the art of aging as early as *Wild Strawberries*. In private he can play an old man with a cane, letting himself be treated as a befuddled senior citizen, because one day he may indeed become one. At the next moment he is bursting with excitement over a project and surprising you with his professional inventiveness and almost manic lust for life. His defiance of physical infirmities suddenly gives a hip injury a biblical dimension. A half-grown beard hints at a drama.

This is not coquetry, either, but a testing of roles, a conquest of experience. A gesture is an instrument of knowledge. The most insignificant everyday habit becomes an act of choosing, an exercise in portrayal — something that can be applied, developed, given a different meaning. The director is at work and life is a stage production. If life slips along pleasantly for a time, you have to find a reason to practice your rage.

Sometimes it is a choice between whether anxiety should chase away sleep or sleep chase away anxiety. Is a well-rested body or a tortured soul the gateway to Strindberg? Both are, of course. Anxiety opens up the text, and the well-rested body provides the strength to portray it. Is illness a chance to give a major project time to mature, or the body's protest against a deadly insight hiding around the corner? Anything is possible. Genuine weariness appears, one can imagine, when Bergman tires of Bergman's drama. These lulls are brief, thank goodness. Soon the search for new, secret vaccines is on once again.

The search for vaccines. Like all the great directors of our age, Bergman has a bit of the scientist and scholar in him. He has eliminated the artificial contradiction between intellect and intuition and has identified new opportunities. I believe that he objects to being termed a scholar. But a thoroughness in text analysis, a search for sources and facts and backgrounds — all this is part of his many irresistibly energetic traits.

His energy and curiosity free his erudition, which he quite honestly denies, from any touch of academism. He is simply knowledgeable. That is part of his craft. You should know everything about the camera and as much as possible about Shakespeare. You should be able to distinguish between different kinds of raw film and between infatuation and love. Everything serves as an instrument of maximal expression.

Being thoroughly familiar with the prerequisites, mechanisms, and possibilities of expression perhaps also requires that you have a command of people and things. Directing is a way of exercising power, even though the rules of the game call on you to deny this. At the edge of power lurks jealousy. Perhaps to impose discipline and order on both jealousy and the pleasures of power, the orderly but anarchistic Bergman has been attracted to major institutions: the municipal theaters of Malmö and Göteborg, the Royal Dramatic Theater, the National Theatre in London, the Residenztheater in Munich, Svensk Filmindustri, the Swedish Film Institute.

As for film, he has of course had his own companies too. To complete the picture, we must add that administration is part of his craft as well. It is also true that Bergman could have become the head of numerous institutions. He has tried that role, but somehow prefers the artist's struggle against an institution to that institution's struggle against national and local governments. He has been tempted by the latter but apparently finds the drain on his energy and adrenaline too taxing on his own work of producing, writing, and directing.

If we wish to squeeze meanings and significance from his behavior, we can of course also say that major institutions are family-like establishments. They offer opportunities for revolt against father figures, for sibling love, familial hierarchies, exercise of authority, good manners, regulated systems of punishment, unexpected rewards, and endless gossip in the nursery. An institution broadens the concept of a family but is recognizable as one.

Broaden and narrow, narrow and broaden while constantly searching for new and surprising recognitions — perhaps this is one way to describe Bergman's work pattern, this calm exercise in restlessness: overpoweringly self-assured in his efforts to overpower insecurity; full of empathy in order to keep his impatience under control; full of

Bengt Ekerot as Death and Max von Sydow as the Knight in The Seventh Seal *(1956)*

impatience in order to keep his empathy under control when it threatens what is required.

Stillness is restrained motion, and the camera is damned well not supposed to go off and do its own thing. It is supposed to stand still until the narrative and expressions threaten to smash it to pieces if it doesn't move a little. The proscenium and the frame around the picture are accepted boundaries and limitations. Precisely for that rea-

son, life throws itself irascibly, expressively, and violently against them. From the movie screen a woman's face talks to us minute after minute, without movement. The screen is a limitation, the picture is a limitation, the body and the face are limitations, yet it all breathes artistic freedom.

All these challenges stimulate the artistic drive that is a necessary prerequisite to such work. It is a matter of constantly battling triviality or equipping triviality with meaning — of giving it dimensions. This is one of the many gateways to Strindberg. This is why Thomas Mann's boring diaries are so fascinating, an exalted form of relaxation. In the end, should we still not dare ask whether God ever has a stomachache? Publicly and in artistic form.

In that case, it might also be a counterweight to all the attempts to monumentalize Bergman. His trivialities in *The Magic Lantern* are also a way of replying to those attacks that try to transform him into some kind of symbol, so that simply by attacking his name someone can throw the spotlight on his own. Doing this does not even require arguments, only a fresh and witty vocabulary. This is sometimes called debate. Meanwhile, the man and his works remain one of Sweden's most outstanding, remarkable instruments for important and living discourse.

Translated by Victor Kayfetz

A LETTER TO INGMAR BERGMAN

MAX VON SYDOW

Max von Sydow appeared continually in Ingmar Berg-man's films from 1957 to 1971, while at the same time forming a mainstay of Bergman's theatrical companies at Hälsingborg and Malmö. This letter was written as part of the special tribute issue of the Swedish film magazine Chaplin, *titled* Ingmar Bergman at 70.

Dear Ingmar,

I needn't remind you of all the obvious things. Yet I am sure that many others will tell about them in detail. I am thinking of all those magic moments on the stage and around the movie camera. Those moments when you made it feel so self-evident to us that we were accomplishing something deeply meaningful and absolutely necessary.

Few directors have shown such trust in their actors, simplified the machinery around them, and emphasized the human being as well as you have. I am deeply grateful to you for all of that — all the way from Jakob to Gregers Werle, from Antonius Block to the prelate, who never materialized. Antonius and his brothers unquestionably changed my life.

And for all the rest — what was neither immortalized by the movie camera nor analyzed by theater critics, what occurred in the shadow of the great drama outside the world of Block and Borg and Vergérus and Winkelman, at a quiet lunch of ham and eggs or at the tea table with the cookie package and the chocolate box; the brief moments that will not be part of history, when we

disrespectfully made fun of both Borg and Vergérus, of Faust and Alceste, of Strindberg and Ibsen — and not least of ourselves. The echo of that laughter can probably still be heard at Hovs Hallar, in Skattungbyn, and on Fårö. Or the evenings off in Malmö when you arranged LP concerts with Bach and Orff on the program and ran films on your private projector: everything from *And Quiet Flows the Don* to *Mister Magoo*. They were also important moments. Over the years their importance has deepened, and I think of them often. That was when the great penguins danced.

Do you remember that one time, on the slope behind the Filmstaden restaurant, when we ended a discussion about life after death by promising each other that the first one who had the opportunity would haunt the other, in all friendliness? I look forward with excitement to that encounter.

Do you remember the bridge we built, Ingmar, early one morning on Fårö, when the water level was too high to enable us to walk with dry shoes out to the wreck in *Through the Glass Darkly?* The light was incredibly beautiful, with

Max von Sydow with Bibi Andersson in a scene from
The Seventh Seal *(1956)*

the morning fog filtering away all shadow and letting the colors of the landscape appear with complete integrity. Everybody helped out, and after an hour and a half the project was finished and we could start filming.

We built a lot of bridges, Ingmar, between ourselves and also to the audience. And you inspired us.

You won't get any flowers from me, but a warm thank you and a kick for good luck with your next bridge. And the next. And the next. . . .

Yours truly,
Max

Translated by Victor Kayfetz

The roles that von Sydow refers to in his letter are Jakob in Ingmar Bergman's production of Vilhelm Moberg's Lea and Rakel *at the Malmö Municipal Theater in 1955; Gregers Werle in Ibsen's* Wild Duck *at the Royal Dramatic Theater in 1972; the knight Antonius Block in* The Seventh Seal, *Johan Borg in* Hour of the Wolf, *Andreas Vergérus in* The Touch *and Andreas Winkelman in* The Passion of Anna.

CONFESSIONS OF A BERGMAN CO-WORKER

GUNNEL LINDBLOM

Gunnel Lindblom's association with Bergman as both stage and screen actress dates back to the 1950s. She appeared in such classics as The Seventh Seal, Wild Strawberries, The Virgin Spring, *and* Winter Light. *She is also the director of the films* Summer Paradise, Sally and Freedom *and* Summer Nights *among others.*

"WE'RE THE BEST OF FRIENDS," SAID KARL-OSKAR TO Kristina in his lilting Småland dialect, in one of the most beautiful declarations of love in Swedish literature.[1]

We have been closely acquainted and have worked together frequently since 1954, Ingmar and I, although actually for me it began even earlier. And it was love at first sight.

I was fifteen years old and had seen Camus's *Caligula* at the Göteborg Municipal Theater. I didn't know what a director *was*, much less that someone named Ingmar Bergman had directed the play. But lightning had struck. I knew that I had to go back to that building on Götaplatsen, that I would have to live my life there. They must have an office, and I could almost type. People like me could sit in the box office and sell tickets.

I wanted in, and I made it three years later when they accepted me as a first-year drama student. I had a special dispensation because I was too young. By then, I knew who Bergman was — and Anders Ek and Ulla Jacobsson and Sven Milliander and Torsten Hammarén.

And Gertrud Fridh! Because of her, I went and saw *The Land of Desire,* but I didn't think much of it. So later, when a friend invited me to see Bergman's latest film, *The Devil's Wanton,* I went reluctantly. I thought Bergman should stick to the *theater* full-time. Swedish movies were bad. To me, the only films that existed were French, with Carné leading the way.

I came out of that movie house reeling like a drunkard, drugged, speechless, with the film rushing through my bloodstream, pumping and thudding. I can still hear the strange tone in Doris Svedlund's voice when she says, "Thomas — my Thomas . . ." I can hear her voice and see her eyes, and I have never dared see the film again. I prefer to remember my feelings. I don't want them corrected by a person who is mature, reflective, analytical, that is, the person I am today.

And I become furious when Ingmar tells me that it was a really bad film! "You can't judge that. You gave it to me almost forty years ago. It shocked me. And no authority, not even you, Ingmar, should try to persuade me that anything was wrong with the way I felt."

Bergman on the set of The Seventh Seal *with Bengt Ekerot (1956)*

My first encounter (although I call it my third) with Bergman was in a long corridor at the Malmö Municipal Theater. I was newly hired, had just arrived, and was thrown headfirst onto the stage for a reading. It was the female leading role in *The Hour of Foolishness* by a dramatist whose name escapes me.[2] A week's rehearsal, but I had made it!

Ingmar walked toward me in the corridor, smiled in a friendly, appreciative way, and said, "You did that role well, damned well — welcome to our theater."

In any event, that was the beginning of several fantastic years in Malmö, where I worked from 1954 to 1959. Ingmar put on thirteen major productions during those five years — one more brilliant than the other, according to the critics. From *The Merry Widow* and the folk musical *Värmlånningarna* to *Don Juan* and *Peer Gynt* to *Le Misanthrope*, Hjalmar Bergman's *Sagan* and *Urfaust*. I had parts in most of them.

The theater was considered the best in the country. Many outstanding performers had been lured south: Åke Fridell, Toivo Pawlo, Gunnar Björnstrand, Gertrud Fridh, Harriet and Bibi Andersson. Later came Ingrid Thulin and Frank Sundström. Some of us became friends for life and are still working together.

In the summers, Ingmar made films like *The Seventh Seal, Wild Strawberries,* and *The Virgin Spring*. Indeed, I don't think I have ever met anyone who has even come close to Ingmar's capacity for work. When did he have time to write his screenplays?

Max von Sydow came down from Helsingborg and joined the ensemble, and of course Ingmar became inordinately fond of this tall, friendly, balky, shy superactor. We had played an unhappy loving couple in Ostrovsky's *The Poor Bride*. We acted well together and liked each other very much; now we would enjoy the thrill of playing the loving couple in Ibsen's *Peer Gynt*.

But it turned out that we were equally shy in the scenes where we were supposed to embrace. I had a new romance, and he was standing and watching in the wings; that made me none the bolder. Anyway, in the play, Solveig is the shy one and Peer the enterprising one.

The premiere was approaching, and our arms had moved no higher than shoulder level. It was unnerving for us to keep on waiting for Ingmar's outburst, because I knew it was coming and that the longer he postponed it, the more dreadful the thunderbolts would be.

"Gunnel and Max, STOP RIGHT THERE!" Here it was. Lots of witnesses on the stage; this play is crawling with actors, all of them undoubtedly superb at playing love scenes. And Bibi had been given the part of one of the dairy maids at the Norwegian mountain chalet. I was going to be replaced, I was sure.

Ingmar marched through the auditorium. It took time. Those 1,800 seats would soon be filled with a cheering audience. Someone else would get to stand there and hug Max.

After an eternity, Ingmar struggled up to the stage. By then I had finished preparing a vigorous speech defending the innocent, inexperienced farm girl, Solveig, who had never been to the movies and seen any Bergman films and therefore could not know how to handle her beloved Peer Gynt.

I didn't get to use my speech, because Ingmar just stood there looking at us warmly, mildly, and for a long time. Then he said, in the most beautiful silky-smooth voice, "Come now. Now let's take it easily and methodically. Gunnel and Max, the two of you should never be closer to each other than one meter. No, actually, two meters. This isn't any damned TV play. Solveig is burning like a torch and Peer has never seen anything like this broad. He doesn't dare approach her, does he, Max? Besides, he's been screwing dairy maids for three days and nights. He doesn't dare get close to *this* kind of love."

Well, after that we stood there burning — two meters apart — for five hours a night and sixty performances in a row.

We worked like mad and enjoyed ourselves enormously. There was no time for private life. Well, once a week we had no performance, because on Tuesdays the symphony orchestra gave concerts on the main stage. That was when a movie-crazed gang of actors gathered at Ingmar's apartment in Erikslust, where he had a *film projector*.

We saw *The Testament of Dr. Mabuse* and *The Blue Angel* again and again, and we devoured early Rossellini, Buñuel, and Fellini. We were in love with Gösta Ekman, Fred Astaire, and Thor Modéen. We saw feature films and shorts; even commercials were welcome.

We discussed content and form, learned a lot about acting, and Ingmar shared his experience, eagerly and generously.

Twenty years later, I was going to direct my first film, *Summer Paradise*. Ingmar was the producer, and it was a week before shooting. We were going to have a final production meeting up at the Film Institute, and twenty film workers and I sat there and waited for him.

But Ingmar didn't show up. I began to worry, because he is pedantically punctual. Katinka, the production manager, arrived with a strange look on her face. She began to read a letter out loud; it wasn't very long: "Dear friends and colleagues. It is terribly sad to have to inform you . . ." I don't remember how it was phrased. It was such an enormous shock.

Ingmar had left Sweden. He had left from Stockholm the day before. His destination was Munich. He was going to settle in Germany. It was awful. Ingmar, who suffered mightily even when he had to spend only a few hours in Copenhagen . . .

Eight years would pass before he was back in Stockholm.

In the old days, Ingmar's temper was more volcanic. He used to refer to anyone who didn't throw furniture around as "inhibited." In his eyes, I was inhibited, and I was happy to let him think so. In fact, I felt it was nice to avoid having my own fits of rage. I preferred conserving my energy for other things. I understood his tantrums, and they didn't scare me. If you relaxed, they dissipated very quickly. He has too much sense of humor to sulk for long.

Well, once he became terribly angry at me. God knows if he has ever really forgiven me.

It was during the filming of *The Silence*. There were complicated, atrociously difficult love scenes (love again!) in the hotel-room bed. Birger Malmsten and I were completely exhausted. But it had apparently worked well. Ingmar was cheery and jolly and was organizing the next scene.

I staggered out toward the studio door to ask for a glass of water. Rulle, the doorman, had heard our furious arguments and said appreciatively "She's a good screamer, that lady in there, what's her name? Siw Malmkvist?"[3]

Anyway, in I went again, ready for the next scene. The floodlights had been moved in sec-

onds. Ingmar met me near the lights and gave me a peculiar look.

"What's that you're wearing?"

"A slip."

"Did you intend to wear it in bed?"

"Don't you like it, Ingmar?"

"No! You're supposed to be naked. In the script, it says Anna is supposed to be NAKED."

That ice-cold look, those penetrating dark eyes. Marik Vos and Sven Nykvist had vanished behind a cabinet. They didn't like it when a hurricane was brewing.

I was trembling badly, hoping it didn't show. Ingmar's outburst didn't materialize. But it will be a long time before I forget the glowing rage in his eyes and the contempt in his voice:

"So what do we do now?!"

"You'll have to find a stand-in, Ingmar."

Why he didn't kill me, I'll never know. . . .

A little later, as I lay there in the bed with my slip on, I heard Ingmar whisper loudly to our makeup man, "What is so f---ing *important* about those hellish goddamned cursed globs of fat?!" I looked down at my breasts, which were rather small, and felt foolish.

Well, why was it so important? A couple of years later I felt I had been unforgivably stupid and prudish. But at the time, I had only one thought in my head: "It's OK to turn my soul inside out, but I want to keep my clothes on."

After that I wasn't in any more films until *Scenes from a Marriage*. But perhaps there were other reasons.

I remember one incident while we were shooting *The Virgin Spring*. We were somewhere deep in the darkest forests of Dalarna province. We were in a hurry, as usual with Ingmar. The last week of exteriors. Would the weather hold? Would the money last? Would we get those sheep in place for the closing sequence of the film?

Everything was meticulously organized. The snow machine with the soap flakes was in place, and the flock of sheep was being held together by a giant lasso that would be pulled away when Ingmar said, "Camera, action!" Then the sun ap-

The Dance of Death, The Seventh Seal *(1956)*

peared. That was not supposed to happen. So the scene was postponed until the following day, which would *have* to be the very last.

That evening I started having awful stomach pains, which I blamed on nerves, or perhaps that chicken we ate for lunch. I managed to find a heating pad to put on my stomach, but I rapidly got worse. They tell me that when several people were trying to carry me to the ambulance, I clung to the bedstead.

I woke up at a hospital in Falun as they were preparing me for surgery. Dazed and furious, I sat up and shouted, "Why?"

"Lie down. Burst appendix. We're in a hurry."

I passed out again — I don't know if it was because of fear or pain, but I remember that I first had time to say, "I won't agree to this. Have you asked *Ingmar Bergman?*" And the hospital staff laughed.

We laughed at that story for a long time, but I felt vaguely ashamed. Was this an expression of belief in authority which I had been unaware of and that slipped out at a moment when my self-censorship was not functioning?

Or was it a reflection of a sense of duty deep inside me: Work comes first and is most impor-tant; private pains, mental or physical, have to wait; stay within budget; don't postpone the premiere; do your job; be prepared.

Oh, Ingmar, how sad, hopeless, impossible, and CRAZY that you won't be making any more films. It's unthinkable, inconceivable.

You have to help us persuade the politicians that serious Swedish cinema is vital, that the Film Institute has to have movie houses all over Sweden, that the people of this country have to be able to see other Swedes up on the silver screen. As you know, we're drowning in pop and Musak and American action movies!

Translated by Victor Kayfetz

Notes

[1] Karl-Oskar and Kristina are the main characters in Vilhelm Moberg's novels *The Emigrants* (1949) and *Unto a Good Land* (1956), which were filmed by Jan Troell in 1969/70 and released in the United States as *The Emigrants* and *The New Land. Ed.*

[2] Her name is Anna Bonacci. *Ed.*

[3] A Swedish revue star and popular singer. *Ed.*

SOME THOUGHTS ABOUT AN OLD COLLEAGUE ON HIS WAY TO CANONIZATION

EVA DAHLBECK

Eva Dahlbeck appeared in six of Ingmar Bergman's films: Secrets of Women, A Lesson in Love, Dreams, Smiles of a Summer Night, Brink of Life, *and* All These Women. *She now devotes her time to her writing career and is the author of more than a dozen novels.*

In recent years Ingmar Bergman has attracted a level of interest that few living individuals ever experience. Not only have his works been the object of endless analyses and dissections, but the man himself has been placed in an intensive spotlight — as if the secret behind the fascination of his works could be discovered in some eccentricity of the master himself. It is a common association and in this case, at least, it may prove justified.

But all this aside, charting a person's works is a less intricate enterprise than charting a person. People have wondered, guessed, listened, deduced, and drawn conclusions, without actually getting any further than a deepening mystification. Like his works, in the end Ingmar Bergman has come to be regarded as a unique phenomenon, many-faceted and impenetrable, sometimes debatable, always controversial.

How has this happened? What is behind this steadily growing, almost hypnotic preoccupation with the artist and his works?

It may be appropriate to compare it with the proverbial snowball, which starts rolling and automatically grows according to some law of physics.

But is it really such a simple mechanism? And even if it were, what got the snowball rolling? What started this accumulating fascination with Ingmar Bergman?

I will make no pretentious attempt here to achieve a categorical solution to this puzzle. As I have indicated, the mechanisms of fascination are often profoundly complex and difficult to pinpoint. The purpose of this exercise is to state some views from the perspective of a colleague and interested fellow human being.

By now many years have passed since I worked with Ingmar Bergman. Without my knowledge, there may have been a lot of changes in his personality as well as in his vision and need for expression. But it would greatly surprise me if there had been any changes in the essentials — in the core of his personality or in his sense of commitment.

There are two sides of Ingmar that strike me as so characteristic that I want to dwell on them just a bit — two sides that may seem contradictory but which in fact are intimately related. I am not talking about any sensational revelations. They are two very well-known facets of his

Eva Dahlbeck as Désirée Armfeldt in Smiles of a Summer Night *(1955)*

character, perhaps viewed here from a slightly unusual perspective: the jester and the god-seeker. These two traits often have a common denominator.

In my opinion, one of Ingmar's most suggestive films is *The Naked Night*.[1] In it he reveals many of his thoughts about the mentality and function of performers. One can venture the guess that these thoughts are applicable to the artistic professions in general. Artists are a breed slightly apart from practical society — a coterie of observers, reflectors, and interpreters who utilize specific qualities apart from purely rational ones, such as imagination, insight, intuition, and a highly developed emotional life — of course aside from their irresistible urge for self-expression. And their rigid sense of mental discipline.

Without such mental discipline, an artist becomes a mere prankster — something completely different from a jester.

The jester is an unmasker, a social critic, a mirror of society. When people laugh at a jester, they are laughing at themselves; when they cry over a jester, they are crying over themselves; and when they hate a jester, they are hating themselves. A jester is a revealer, a scourger, and an incurable lover of people. Jesters love and want to be loved by everybody.

I imagine that Ingmar Bergman still is and still wants to be a jester and live with jesters, as he did when we worked together. In the middle of his critique of society's often monstrous mechanisms, in the middle of his desperation, his skepticism, indeed in the middle of his cynicism, he seemed to me to be driven by love. Love of his work, his colleagues, his audience. Love of the very life that had been violated. And that impression persists. His love sees both the comedy and the tragedy in the human condition, both its hopelessness and its hopefulness. His reflections give expression to the different facets of life so that we can hardly distinguish them from each other. And his drawing power over our senses can most likely be explained at least partly by the lovingness of his portrayals, by the sense of human solidarity that may lie at the root of all his efforts. Perhaps at times this love has seemed cryptic or less than well articulated.

To me, Ingmar Bergman seems the born jester, with all the powers of insight this implies: insight into the ways and paradoxes of the world, the human soul and its conflicts; the sorrow and disgust, anger and revolt that jesting signifies, and the love it entails; above all, the drive to reflect, describe, frighten, amuse, awaken — in a word, the drive to communicate — that this role implies.

But will people allow him to be a jester? I have wondered in recent years. Isn't there an inherent danger in the gap that has been created between Ingmar Bergman and the great mass of individuals? Isn't there a risk that the world he describes will seem unreal, apart, the child of the increasingly exclusive and sophisticated imagination of a brilliant eccentric? Isn't there a danger in the increasingly categorical demands on this eccentric — demands for originality, sensationalism, and above all a kind of papal infallibility in the artistic realm?

Isn't there a risk that his being put on such a pedestal may hamper the freedom of inquiry? The flow of inspiration should be allowed to follow its own pathways, while perhaps not always obeying the traffic signs of inflated expectations. Indeed, at times inspiration should be allowed to get sidetracked during its always dangerous journey, without any grave diggers standing ready with their shovels.

I am not arguing that such a danger exists, but am merely posing a question — a thought from among the ranks of those jesters who are still roaming freely. The press has the power actively to stop an artist, or to kill him with silence. But doesn't it also have the power to tie him hand and foot through overexploitation?

As I say, I am merely asking. I feel on safer ground when I move on to the identification between jester and god-seeker.

Just as people need their jesters, they need their god-seekers. Not least in our age is there a crying need for both, given the doomsday depression that has spread beneath our empty heaven. To whom can people turn — on the one hand to find spokesmen for their anxieties and on the other to find diversion from these anxieties — if not to their jesters? And where can they find the god they need and dare to believe in?

Of course the church would be the logical tour guide on such a journey of discovery. But, as we all know, the church has become trapped between tradition and science: between anachronistic, mutually contradictory interpretations of the Bible and mystifications and a rational view of the world. At least for the time being, the church is hanging in midair. People have to find slightly firmer ground on which to seek the life sources they will ultimately depend upon. More than ever, they need unmaskers, reflectors, interpreters. They need those capable of lighting up and making fun of untruths — in order thereby to reveal some little morsel of truth, no matter how hypothetical and ambiguous.

Jesters have always been truth-seekers, following the path of antithesis. And in the end, this truth cannot reasonably be anything but the truth about God.

In this way we often find conscious or unconscious god-seekers among artists, especially those with the temperament of Ingmar Bergman the jester. Although his own specific explorations, admittedly, possess an uncommon frenzy and provocativeness, Bergman's spiritual curiosity seems boundless. And here we finally arrive at a third and equally well-known Bergman character trait, which in turn is closely associated with the two mentioned above. One can even ask whether both

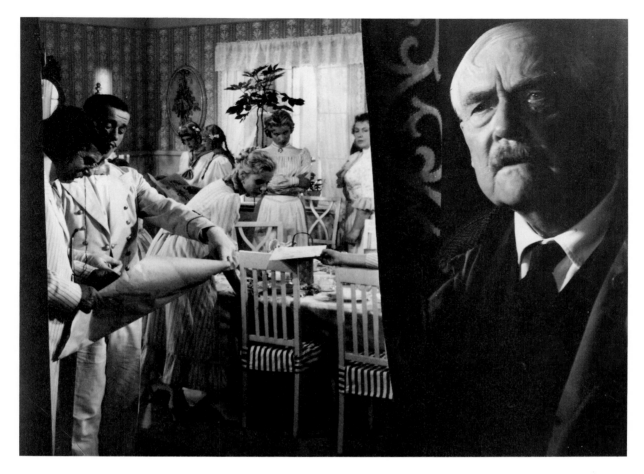

Victor Sjöström (right) remembering the past in Wild
Strawberries *(1957)*

the jester and the god-seeker have their deepest
roots somewhere in this third and, in one sense,
overriding identity — Ingmar Bergman the eroticist.

Once again, I must disappoint those who are
hoping for some as yet unpublished insight into
Ingmar's highly private love life, because on that
point I am undoubtedly more poorly informed
than many of my readers. When I speak of eroticism here, it is not in the most narrow sense of the
word but, rather, in its broadest — an attraction
to and sense of union with existence as a whole. I
am speaking of the role of eroticism in the overall
scheme of things.

I will permit myself to quote a few lines from

my just-completed novel, which touches on the
erotic dimension I am referring to:

Perhaps it sounds strange, but I believe that
David has an erotic relationship with everything around him — with nature, people,
things, indeed with everything that happens.
It may appear as if he is involved in some
universal act of love that is sometimes fruitful and sometimes destructive. But he seems
unable, or unwilling, to free himself from the
attachment, the attraction and sensation of
pleasure that unites him with all living
things. One can easily get the impression of a
kind of uninterrupted ecstasy — low-keyed,

slow-burning, like an electric current. It is a fire that drives him in everything, even as he looks for the key to human life, the sense of order he cannot get out of his mind. . . . Now I understand better what he means by religion. His religion has hardly any connection with what he refers to as sanctified bureaucracies, nor is it something ethereal or abstract. His religion is presence and concreteness; it is a kind of relationship, or indeed an integration with all of creation. He feels involved in everything that happens, he feels responsible for everything that happens. His religion exists in all his feelings, in his spiritual search, as well as his sexuality.

This is no *roman à clef,* any more than other novels in which an author borrows material from his or her personal experiences and encounters with people. David is not identical with Ingmar Bergman. But it is true that Ingmar was certainly one of the two central figures I had in mind when I struggled with my David, who in turn represents an increasingly penetrating approach to God — one that combines science with the paths of spiritual knowledge, one that moves the creative vital force right into reality.

Given this alteration in concepts, we cannot avoid also extending the concept of sexuality almost ad infinitum. Eroticism becomes part of the very texture of life and may be strongly or less strongly expressed in individuals. Just as I, in a highly personal way, have understood Ingmar Bergman to be an eroticist in the broadest sense of the word.

Of course, I am fully aware that my analysis may be debatable or even totally off the wall. In that case I am not only prepared but also eager to be corrected by someone who knows better. These thoughts are ultimately based on a personal conviction about the responsibility of jesters: about people's need for a few public figures who commit themselves to their cause without opportunistic side-glances, political or otherwise — people's need for the incorrigible love found behind the jester's sometimes savage and bitter reflections. I have the impression that Ingmar is one of those who is unusually well equipped to fill such a need in people, and that it may possibly be the dimension of human solidarity in his works that first set the ball rolling.

If this should be the case, I only hope that Ingmar Bergman is able to shake off his papal infallibility. I hope he can continue working with that motley brotherhood or sisterhood who eagerly, obstinately, and with varying success strive to portray the cruel, grotesque (and at blessed moments, heavenly and wonderful) state of earthly life.

Ingmar once coined the nickname "Battleship of Femininity" for me. It was an epithet that I clearly managed to live up to in the roles he assigned to me, but which I have considerable difficulty fulfilling in private life. I see this as a good example of the jester's ability to reflect observed reality to the point of confusion. In other words, to recognize and mobilize in oneself one of the innumerable needs of personality that lie imbedded in the human psyche, temporarily enlarging it and experiencing its life.

So I hope that my impressions of an old colleague are not based on some temporary set of reflections, but on the master's genuine personality.

Translated by Victor Kayfetz

Note

[1] The Swedish title, *Gycklarnas afton,* literally means "Night of the Jesters." *Trans.*

BERGMAN ON STAGE AND SCREEN:
EXCERPTS FROM A SEMINAR WITH *BIBI ANDERSSON*

Bibi Andersson's 1990s appearances in several of Ingmar Bergman's productions at the Royal Dramatic Theater continue a long collaboration that began with his films of the 1950s. These include The Seventh Seal, Wild Strawberries, Persona, *and* Scenes from a Marriage. *This seminar, sponsored by the American Film Institute, took place in 1977.*

QUESTION: The hazards of film work must sometimes make you long for the theater. You were, after all, trained for the theater, and you've often appeared with the Royal Dramatic Theater in Stockholm. Do you intend to go on moving back and forth between theater and film as Bergman himself has done?

ANDERSSON: I love the theater I have been with. The problem is that if you are with that theater you have to be there twelve months a year. There is no such thing as leaving and coming back for guest appearances. I have tried to take half a year off and play the rest of the year, but it created so much jealousy, I decided that since I don't want to be tied up by the theater for twelve months a year — I feel imprisoned a little bit — I had to choose, and so I have left the theater. It hurts. I would have liked to be able to do both, but that kind of jealousy is very hard in Sweden, and it's even a drawback to have been abroad. Unless you come back as Greta Garbo, you're not worth very much, and it's sometimes frustrating. I had gone back to do *Twelfth Night*. Bergman wanted me to do it.

I played it, but all the actors had a meeting. The result of that meeting was that neither I nor Max von Sydow should be allowed to come back again and play. A full commitment was required. There were so many girls for the parts. I can understand that. If you are in a theater and you work in all different parts, and all of a sudden somebody comes home and just nibbles and takes the best thing, it's very frustrating.

QUESTION: But you're not giving up the theater?

ANDERSSON: No, I will try to find other places to act.

QUESTION: Do you respond differently to a stage play compared to a screenplay? Does quality or the absence of quality matter more in one form than in the other?

ANDERSSON: A bad play will always be a bad play, no matter how much of a genius the director is, because there are certain things that the dialogue cannot cover. You cannot have a close-up and cover up what is said so loud that everybody is supposed to hear it. But a bad script can turn out to be a very good movie if the director

Bibi Andersson, Liv Ullmann, Sven Nykvist, and Ing-
mar Bergman taking a break during the filming of
Persona *(1965)*

has a very imaginative mind. He sees things and makes choices. So usually I don't judge a film script from what I read. I have to judge it from the way the director talks about it, from what he tells me he would like to do, or why he sees me in the part. I have to be seduced into it, or at least I have to seduce myself if nobody else does, if I really want to do it. But I cannot say that I've ever read a film script and said, "Oh, that is such great literature."

QUESTION: Then you would consider that screenwriting is not as important for filmmaking as the work of the dramatist is for the theater?

ANDERSSON: Bergman, when he writes a script, writes it as a novel, and you know that whatever he writes will be in the film one way or another. He writes in such a way that you get seduced, you get ideas. But other writers write lines, and whatever is supposed to take place between those lines is a secret between the writer and the director. Anyway, it's not written in the script that they give me to read. It's difficult to know how their minds are going to work. Maybe it's just that I am not used to reading American scripts, but I find them usually very flat. It troubles me because I don't know how to read them or to ask the right questions about them.

QUESTION: Bergman has said that what he does in a film sometimes is determined by what he knows of the actor or actress he wants. Have you found that?

ANDERSSON: Yes. I have a feeling that it's mostly when he's writing or when he's casting that Bergman gives his direction. I don't know, now that he's going to do films out of Sweden, what kind of commercial aspects he has to have in mind. But I know that, before, it was the knowledge of a person that inspired him to

Bergman in conference with cinematographer Sven Nykvist

write in a certain direction. Even if it was unconscious, I'm sure it was playing a big part. If
he was at work on something and knew that
one of his actress friends had a similar problem
or attitude, he would use her. When I was reading a script, I tried to figure out what side of me
he was trying to use now, or what had he seen,
or what it was that he did not want. You can
sometimes be very frustrated if you feel the part
does not do you justice. When I read *Persona* I
wasn't flattered. I didn't understand why I had
to play this sort of insecure, weak personality
when I was struggling so hard to be sure of
myself and to cover up my insecurities. I realized that he was totally aware of my personality. I was better off just trying to deliver
that. It's a good way to know oneself. Sometimes I think artists instinctively are very good
psychiatrists. I also think all parts have to be
based on oneself, otherwise they will never
come across.

QUESTION: What sort of environment does Bergman create on the set that allows you to flow in
your acting?

ANDERSSON: You have to create that for yourself.
But he has to create an environment of concentration — it has to be quiet on the set; he
doesn't want intruders or visitors. Yet sometimes he creates a mood that frightens people;
you need to be very tense, and the discipline
can be quite tough. That might be very good in
certain respects, but it can be easier to work
with other directors, who are looser and more
insecure themselves. They can help you to just
go ahead with whatever you have. If you laugh
or if you do wrong, it will not be interpreted as
lack of discipline, which sometimes happens
with him. But during filming for Bergman, the
most important thing you feel is that everybody, including, of course, Bergman himself, is
focusing on what you are doing in relation to
the camera — and that's important.

QUESTION: Some of your most memorable work
was done in early Bergman films — *The Seventh Seal, Wild Strawberries*. That's some

Split image of Bibi Andersson and Liv Ullmann, Persona *(1965)*

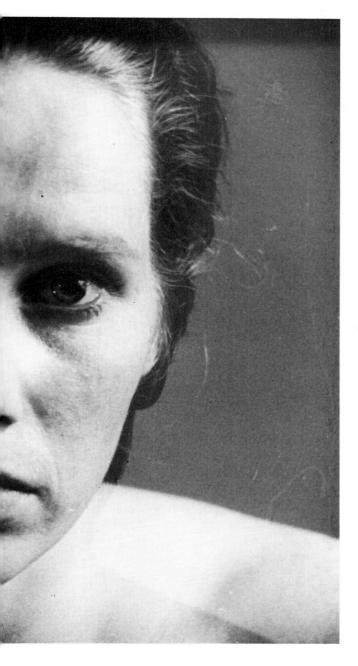

twenty years ago. What's your attitude today toward those films and your work in them?

ANDERSSON: I don't feel anything for my work in those films. I love the films, still. They are very vivid in my memory even if they're twenty years old. But I have no connection with what I was doing then. I saw *Wild Strawberries* recently, and I thought I was terrible, terrible. But we were all rather corny in those days. There was a certain kind of acting that seemed different, or perhaps it had to do with the sound that came out different. I don't know. The voices sounded different then; I hear them as being artificial. Maybe that is why I feel a certain distance when I see those films.

But it doesn't matter. I'm proud of the films, but not with regard to myself. *Persona,* on the other hand, I'm still proud of. Each time I see it, I know I accomplished what I set out to do as an actress, that I created a person.

QUESTION: Would you say that film represented the difference between youthful work and mature work?

ANDERSSON: I think so, yes.

QUESTION: What survives very well from those films is a quality of innocence in your characters — particularly in *The Seventh Seal,* in which the character is almost madonna-like.

ANDERSSON: When I was very young I had a certain kind of innocence that, unluckily enough, life has not let me keep. I was innocent in the sense that I was very trustful, I loved people, I loved life. But I was not shy. I was outgoing. I was myself in those clothes in *The Seventh Seal,* and I think it came out. When I see it today, I think it's beautiful. In those days, I was not being conscious of what I was doing. I was just trying to be natural.

My part in *Wild Strawberries* is much more complicated. I understood it all later. I remembered so well that Bergman wanted me to bring out something I wasn't aware of in the dream scene in the woods when I am holding the mirror in front of the old man. He said, "You are youthful and cruel. Because of your innocence you have no pity. Because of the way you are — happy, outgoing, curious — you judge and condemn people. All those young, beautiful qualities in certain situations are very brutal. Remember that." He meant that at the same time that the young can be very charming, they can also be very tactless. They can say, "You are no good. What did you do with your life?" It's so easy to say such things when you haven't given your own life a try. He wanted me to project that kind of sudden coldness that a young person can have — coldness without pity.

It was a very interesting part, and I understood what Bergman was saying. But I'm not at all sure I knew how to play it. That's why I was disappointed when I saw *Wild Strawberries* again. Realizing what a great part it was, I didn't think I measured up to it.

QUESTION: Could you play that part today?

ANDERSSON: I would play it totally differently. I would not be able to play a certain kind of absolute freshness — of course. I could always act it, but today I would make different choices. I remember when I was rehearsing *Twelfth Night* for the stage with Bergman. I was going to do Viola. At first, we were just playing, and he said, "It's so wonderful. You never change." I started to work on the role, and I worked and worked. He said, "The more you work, the worse it gets. This part is not that complicated. Just try to remember who you were twenty years ago. Play that. With what you have achieved since, that'll be fine. Just go ahead and be happy and don't think." The nights I succeeded in doing that, I was good. But certain nights when I was too aware or conscious, I was less spontaneous. Acting is so fascinating when there is that mixture of being aware and of just letting yourself be innocent.

QUESTION: Your role in *Persona* is the one most often discussed, and there are any number of scenes worth discussing. For example, the strongly erotic scene in which you tell Liv Ullmann about a sexual encounter with two boys on a beach. It's a long close-up on you, it's all talk, but Pauline Kael has called it one of the most erotic moments in cinema. How did you bring it about?

ANDERSSON: I'll tell you technically what happened. Bergman wanted to cut that scene. His wife had read it or — I don't know — but he was advised not to keep it in. I said, "Let me shoot it, but just let me alter certain words no woman would say. It's written by a man, and I can feel it's a man. Let me change certain things." He said, "You do what you want with it. We'll shoot it, and then we'll go and see it together."

He was very embarrassed and so was I — I was terribly embarrassed to do the scene. We shot it in one long close-up in one take. Two hours. We started rehearsing at nine, and we were through at eleven. There was both Liv's and my own close-up. Then we saw it, and he said, "I'll keep it. It's so good. But I want you, all by yourself, to go into the dubbing room, because there's something wrong with the sound." I didn't think so. I had been talking very high, very girlish. So the whole monologue was dubbed afterward, and I changed my voice. I suddenly put my voice lower, and that I dared to do when I was totally alone and no one could watch me or see me or anything. That might be what gives the scene a certain intimate quality. But I never had that dream.

QUESTION: There is another scene — a gray, twilight scene — when you and Liv Ullmann meet in a room, and you seem to melt into each other. How did you approach that?

ANDERSSON: I remember the studio was full of smoke because it was going to be this kind of blurry thing. Ingmar had a mirror, and we also knew that one of the big problems with the shooting was how to compose the frames, when there were only two people all the time, without just having a reverse over one shoulder. How do you make us move in the same shots so that it will still have movement and be interesting and not boring? He wanted a mirror. He said, "It will be very beautiful." He also

Bibi Andersson (front) and Liv Ullmann in a scene from Persona *(1965)*

said, "Move and we'll see." So we moved. Liv pulled my hair back, and I took her hair. We didn't know what to do, and we just tried to make the frame look interesting. Finally he said, "That's it," and they shot it.

QUESTION: What do you make of *Persona*'s ending? You've spent a period of time at the shore with Liv Ullmann as the patient and you as the nurse, and now you board a bus.

ANDERSSON: For me it meant returning to my life and world and that she was going back to hers. This was a meeting from two universes; they overlapped. I came out having gained a certain experience, and, hopefully, she with another. But as usual in life, what we have experienced, what might have changed us inside, doesn't necessarily change the whole outside. We had just maybe gotten one new insight, one new approach to things. But we had borrowed the house for two months, and the time was up.

She went first, back to the hospital. I had to go back to the hospital, too, where I would continue my services as a nurse. Being the nurse, I was the servant, and I stayed to clean up the house. I remember I had terribly ugly rubber shoes on. I could hardly walk in them — and that ugly hat.

QUESTION: I think some people might be disappointed with such an interpretation of the ending, wanting something more profound.

ANDERSSON: I think that for a while the two women really mingled, that I as a nurse understood something. Without explanation, I came very, very close to this woman. I understood her. I identified with her, and I was even able to say things in her place. I'm sure all this will change the life of the nurse, because before that she had been very square. She had never used her imagination toward other people; she had never analyzed what was happening to herself either. Suddenly, through the silence of the other woman, she was able to put herself in her place, understanding her world and her thinking and to express that.

QUESTION: Sven Nykvist has been Bergman's photographer for most of his films. What relationship have you formed with him on the set?

ANDERSSON: Sven is a very shy and timid person. Lately, because he has gotten used to traveling and talking to people, he has started to talk much more. But when I used to work with him, he said about ten words to me during the whole shooting. What I felt from him was a great warmth. But sometimes if I was having a big fight with Ingmar, he would say, "Yes, go on," though he wouldn't dare have one himself. Sven and I and Erland Josephson, who played in *Scenes from a Marriage* and *Face to Face,* recently finished a film for television without a director. Erland wrote the script, and he and Sven formed a production company, and I participated. We said, "Why don't we try to see how much we really contribute ourselves? Why do we need to talk to a director and explain to him what we want to do?" It was an experiment. We found out we needed a director. We liked one another so much that Sven was not capable of telling us that we acted badly, and whenever he asked me to look in the camera to see if I liked the framing, I was so flattered that I just said, "That is so beautiful." Maybe it will come out nice anyway, because we liked what we were doing. I haven't seen it yet.

QUESTION: In all the years you worked with Bergman, something of a repertory atmosphere developed with such other performers as Liv Ullmann and Max von Sydow. Many moviegoers must regard you as part of almost a family of very skilled actors. Do you in fact feel closer to Ullmann and von Sydow and others than to actors from other films?

ANDERSSON: Max and Liv, yes, I feel very close to them. I know how they think, I know how they work. This said, I can communicate as well with other people. If you arrive on a new set and work with new actors, everybody always makes an effort to find a means of communication. That is the common denominator between all actors.

PART FOUR

REFLECTIONS ON BERGMAN

THE NORTHERN PROTESTANT

JAMES BALDWIN

James Baldwin, the distinguished American novelist, essayist, and playwright, traveled to Stockholm to interview Ingmar Bergman for this essay, which first appeared in Esquire *in 1961 and was later reprinted in Baldwin's* Nobody Knows My Name.

I ALREADY KNEW THAT BERGMAN HAD JUST COMPLETED one movie, was mixing the sound for it, and was scheduled to begin another almost at once. When I called the Filmstaden, he himself, incredibly enough, came to the phone. He sounded tired but very pleasant and told me he could see me if I came at once.

The Filmstaden is in a suburb of Stockholm called Rasunda, and is the headquarters of Svensk Filmindustri, which is one of the oldest movie companies in the world. It was here that Victor Sjöström made those remarkable movies which eventually (under the name Victor Seastrom) carried him — briefly — to the arid plains of Hollywood. Here Mauritz Stiller directed *The Story of Gösta Berling,* after which he and the star thus discovered, Garbo, also took themselves west — a disastrous move for Stiller and not, as it was to turn out, altogether the most fruitful move, artistically anyway, that Garbo could have made. Ingrid Bergman left here in 1939. (She is not related to Ingmar Bergman.) The Svensk Filmindustri is proud of these alumni, but they are prouder of no one, at the moment, than they are of Ingmar Berg-

man, whose films have placed the Swedish film industry back on the international map. And yet, on the whole, they take a remarkably steady view of the Bergman vogue. They realize that it *is* a vogue, they are bracing themselves for the inevitable reaction, and they hope that Bergman is doing the same. He is neither as great nor as limited as the current hue and cry suggests. But he is one of the very few genuine artists now working in films.

He is also, beyond doubt, the freest. Not for him the necessity of working on a shoestring, with unpaid performers, as has been the case with many of the younger French directors. He is backed by a film company; Swedish film companies usually own their laboratories, studios, rental distribution services, and theaters. If they did not they could scarcely afford to make movies at all, movies being more highly taxed in this tiny country than anywhere else in the world — except Denmark — and sixty percent of the playing time in these company-owned theaters being taken up by foreign films. Nor can the Swedish film industry possibly support anything resembling the American star system. This is healthy for the performers, who never have to sit idly by for a couple of years, waiting for a fat part, and who are able to develop a range and flexibility rarely permitted even to the most gifted of our stars. And, of course, it's fine for Bergman because he is absolutely free to choose his own performers: if he wishes to work, say, with Geraldine Page, studio pressure will not force him into extracting a performance from Kim Novak. If it were not for this freedom we would almost certainly never have heard of Ingmar Bergman. Most of his twenty-odd movies were not successful when they were made, nor are they today his company's biggest money-makers. (His vogue has changed this somewhat, but, as I say, no one expects this vogue to last.) "He wins the prizes and brings us the prestige," was the comment of one of his co-workers, "but it's So-and-So and So-and-So" — and here he named two very popular Swedish directors — "who can be counted on to bring in the money."

I arrived at the Filmstaden a little early; Bergman was still busy and would be a little late in meeting me, I was told. I was taken into his office to wait for him. I welcomed the opportunity of seeing the office without the man.

It is a very small office, most of it taken up by a desk. The desk is placed smack in front of the window — not that it could have been placed anywhere else; this window looks out on the daylight landscape of Bergman's movies. It was gray and glaring the first day I was there, dry and fiery. Leaves kept falling from the trees, each silent descent bringing a little closer the long, dark Swedish winter. The forest Bergman's characters are always traversing is outside this window and the ominous carriage from which they have yet to escape is still among the properties. I realized, with a small shock, that the landscape of Bergman's mind was simply the landscape in which he had grown up.

On the desk were papers, folders, a few books, all very neatly arranged. Squeezed between the desk and the wall was a spartan cot; a brown leather jacket and brown knitted cap were lying on it. The visitor's chair in which I sat was placed at an angle to the door, which proximity, each time that I was there, led to much bumping and scraping and smiling exchanges in Esperanto. On the wall were three photographs of Charlie Chaplin and one of Victor Sjöström.

Eventually, he came in, bareheaded, wearing a sweater, a tall man, economically, intimidatingly lean. He must have been the gawkiest of adolescents, his arms and legs still seeming to be very loosely anchored; something in his good-natured, self-possessed directness suggests that he would also have been among the most belligerently opinionated: by no means an easy man to deal with, in any sense, any relationship whatever, there being about him the evangelical distance of someone possessed by a vision. This extremely dangerous quality — authority — has never failed to incite the hostility of the many. And I got the impression that Bergman was in the habit of saying what he felt because he knew that scarcely anyone was listening.

He suggested tea, partly, I think, to give both of us time to become easier with each other, but also because he really needed a cup of tea before going back to work. We walked out of the office and down the road to the canteen.

I had arrived in Stockholm with what turned out to be the "flu" and I kept coughing and sneezing and wiping my eyes. After a while Bergman began to look at me worriedly and said that I sounded very ill.

I hadn't come there to talk about my health and I tried to change the subject. But I was shortly to learn that any subject changing to be done around Bergman is done by Bergman. He was not to be sidetracked.

"Can I do anything for you?" he persisted; and when I did not answer, being both touched and irritated by his question, he smiled and said, "You haven't to be shy. I know what it is like to be ill and alone in a strange city."

It was a hideously, an inevitably self-conscious gesture and yet it touched and dis-

Scene from Through a Glass Darkly *(1960)*

armed me. I know that his concern, at bottom, had very little to do with me. It had to do with his memories of himself and it expressed his determination never to be guilty of the world's indifference.

He turned and looked out of the canteen window, at the brilliant October trees and the glaring sky, for a few seconds and then turned back to me.

"Well," he asked me, with a small laugh, "are you for me or against me?"

I did not know how to answer this question right away and he continued, "I don't care if you are or not. Well, that's not true. Naturally, I prefer — I would be happier — if you were *for* me. But I have to know."

I told him I was for him, which might, indeed, turn out to be my principal difficulty in writing about him. I had seen many of his movies — but did not intend to try to see them all — and I felt identified, in some way, with what I felt he was trying to do. What he saw when he looked at the world did not seem very different from what *I* saw. Some of his films seemed rather cold to me, somewhat too deliberate. For example, I had possibly heard too much about *The Seventh Seal* before seeing it, but it had impressed me less than some of the others.

"I cannot discuss that film," he said abruptly, and again turned to look out of the window. "I had to do it. I had to be free of that argument, those questions." He looked at me. "It's the same for you when you write a book? You just do it because you must and then, when you have done it, you are relieved, no?"

He laughed and poured some tea. He had made it sound as though we were two urchins playing a deadly and delightful game which must be kept a secret from our elders.

"Those questions?"

"Oh. God and the Devil. Life and Death. Good and Evil." He smiled. "*Those* questions."

I wanted to suggest that his being a pastor's son contributed not a little to his dark preoccupations. But I did not quite know how to go about digging into his private life. I hoped that we would be able to do it by way of the movies.

I began with: "The question of love seems to occupy you a great deal, too."

I don't doubt that it occupies you, too, was what he seemed to be thinking, but he only said, mildly, "Yes." Then, before I could put it another way, "You may find it a bit hard to talk to me. I really do not see much point in talking about my past work. And I cannot talk about work I haven't done yet."

I mentioned his great preoccupation with egotism, so many of his people being centered on themselves, necessarily, and disastrously: Vogler in *The Magician,* Isak Borg in *Wild Strawberries,* the ballerina in *Summer Interlude* [*Illicit Interlude* in U.S.*].

"I am very fond of *Summer Interlude,*" he said. "It is my favorite movie."

"I don't mean," he added, "that it's my best. I don't know which movie is my best."

Summer Interlude was made in 1950. It is probably not Bergman's best movie — I would give that place to the movie which has been shown in the States as *The Naked Night* — but it is certainly among the most moving. Its strength lies in its portrait of the ballerina, uncannily precise and truthful, and in its perception of the nature of first love, which first seems to open the universe to us and then seems to lock us out of it. It is one of the group of films — including *Waiting Women* [*Secrets of Women*], *Smiles of a Summer Night,* and *Brink of Life* — which have a woman, or women, at their center and in which the men, generally, are rather shadowy. But all the Bergman themes are in it: his preoccupation with time and the inevitability of death, the comedy of human entanglements, the nature of illusion, the nature of egotism, the price of art. These themes also run through the movies which have at their center a man: *The Naked Night* (which should really be called *The Clown's Evening*), *Wild Strawberries, The Face* [*The Magician*], *The Seventh Seal*. In only one of these movies — *The Face* — is the male-female relation affirmed from the male point of view; as being, that is, a source of strength for the man. In the movies concerned with women, the male-female relation succeeds only through the passion, wit, or patience of the woman and depends on how astutely she is able to manipulate the male conceit. *The Naked Night* is the most blackly ambivalent of Bergman's films — and surely one of the most brutally erotic movies ever made — but it is essentially a study of the masculine helplessness before the female force. *Wild Strawberries* is inferior to it, I think, being afflicted with a verbal and visual rhetoric which is Bergman's most annoying characteristic. But the terrible assessments that the old Professor is forced to make in it prove that he is not merely

Ingmar Bergman with actor Gunnar Björnstrand during the filming of Winter Light *(1961/62)*

the victim of his women: he is responsible for what his women have become.

We soon switched from Bergman's movies to the subject of Stockholm.

"It is not a city at all," he said, with intensity. "It is ridiculous of it to think of itself as a city. It is simply a rather larger village, set in the middle of some forests and some lakes. You wonder what it thinks it is doing there, looking so important."

I was to encounter in many other people this curious resistance to the idea that Stockholm could possibly become a city. It certainly seemed to be trying to become a city as fast as it knew how, which is, indeed, the natural and inevitable fate of any nation's principal commercial and cul-

grinding out the inevitable rock-and-roll tunes, and there are, too, a few jazz joints which fail, quite, to remind one of anything in the States. And the ghost — one is tempted to call it the effigy — of the late James Dean complete with uniform, masochistic girl friend, motorcycle, or (hideously painted) car, has made its appearance on the streets of Stockholm. These do not frighten me nearly as much as the originals in New York, since they have yet to achieve the authentic American bewilderment or the inimitable American snarl. I ought to add, perhaps, that the American Negro remains, for them, a kind of *monstre sacré,* which proves, if anything does, how little they know of the phenomena which they feel compelled to imitate. They are unlike their American models in many ways: for example, they are not suffering from a lack of order but from an excess of it. Sexually, they are not drowning in taboos; they are anxious, on the contrary, to establish one or two.

But the people in Stockholm are right to be frightened. It is not Stockholm's becoming a city which frightens them. What frightens them is that the pressures under which everyone in this century lives are destroying the old simplicities. This is almost always what people really mean when they speak of Americanization. It is an epithet which is used to mask the fact that the entire social and moral structure that they have built is proving to be absolutely inadequate to the demands now being placed on it. The old cannot imagine a new one, or create it. The young have no confidence in the old; lacking which, they cannot find any standards in themselves by which to live. The most serious result of such a chaos, though it may not seem to be, is the death of love. I do not mean merely the bankruptcy of the concept of romantic love — it is entirely possible that this concept has had its day — but the breakdown of communication between the sexes.

tural clearinghouse. But for Bergman, who is forty-one, and for people who are considerably younger, Stockholm seems always to have had the aspect of a village. They do not look forward to seeing it change. Here, as in other European towns and cities, people can be heard bitterly complaining about the "Americanization" which is taking place.

This "Americanization," so far as I could learn, refers largely to the fact that more and more people are leaving the countryside and moving into Stockholm. Stockholm is not prepared to receive these people, and the inevitable social tensions result, from housing problems to juvenile delinquency. Of course, there are jukeboxes

Bergman talked a little about the early stages of his career. He came to the Filmstaden in 1944, when he wrote the script for *Torment*. This was a very promising beginning. But promising beginnings do not mean much, especially in the movies. Promise, anyway, was never what Bergman lacked. He lacked flexibility. Neither he nor anyone else I talked to suggested that he has since acquired much of this quality; and since he was young and profoundly ambitious and thoroughly untried, he lacked confidence. This lack he disguised by tantrums so violent that they are still talked about at the Filmstaden today. His exasperating allergies extended to such things as refusing to work with a carpenter, say, to whom he had never spoken but whose face he disliked. He has been known, upon finding guests at his home, to hide himself in the bathroom until they left. Many of these people never returned and it is hard, of course, to blame them. Nor was he, at this time in his life, particularly respectful of the feelings of his friends.

"He's improved," said a woman who has been working with him for the last several years, "but he was impossible. He could say the most terrible things, he could make you wish you were dead. Especially if you were a woman."

She reflected. "Then, later, he would come and apologize. One just had to accept it, that's all."

He was referred to in those days, without affection, as "the young one" or "the kid" or "the demon director." An American property whose movies, in spite of all this temperament, made no money at the box office, would have suffered, at best, the fate of Orson Welles. But Bergman went on working, as screenwriter and director in films and as a director on the stage.

"I was an actor for a while," he says, "a terribly bad actor. But it taught me much."

It probably taught him a great deal about how to handle actors, which is one of his great gifts.

He directed plays for the municipal theaters of Hälsingborg, Göteborg, and Malmö, and is now working — or will be as soon as he completes his present film schedule — for the Royal Dramatic Theater of Stockholm.

Some of the people I met told me that his work on stage is even more exciting than his work in films. They were the same people, usually, who were most concerned for Bergman's future when his present vogue ends. It was as though they were giving him an ace in the hole.

I did not interrogate Bergman on this point, but his record suggests that he is more attracted to films than to the theater. It would seem, too, that the theater very often operates for him as a kind of prolonged rehearsal or preparation for a film already embryonic in his consciousness. This is almost certainly the case with at least two of his theatrical productions. In 1954, he directed for the municipal theater of Malmö, Franz Lehár's *The Merry Widow*. The next year he wrote and directed the elaborate period comedy *Smiles of a Summer Night*, which beautifully utilizes — for Bergman's rather savage purposes — the atmosphere of romantic light opera. In 1956, he published his play *A Medieval Fresco* [Wood Painting]. This play was not produced, but it forms the basis for *The Seventh Seal*, which he wrote and directed the same year. It is safe, I think, to assume that the play will now never be produced, at least not by Bergman.

He has had many offers, of course, to work in other countries. I asked him if he had considered taking any of them.

He looked out of the window again. "I am home here," he said. "It took me a long time, but now I have all my instruments — everything — where I want them. I know my crew, my crew knows me, I know my actors."

I watched him. Something in me, inevitably, envied him for being able to love his home so directly and for being able to stay at home and work. And, in another way, rather to my surprise, I envied him not at all. Everything in a life depends on how that life accepts its limits: it would have been like envying him his language.

"If I were a violinist," he said after a while, "and I were invited to play in Paris — well, if the condition was that I could not bring my own violin but would have to play a French one — well, then, I could not go." He made a quick gesture toward the window. "This is my violin."

It was getting late. I had the feeling that I should be leaving, though he had not made any

Gunnel Lindblom with Jörgen Lindström and Ingrid Thulin in The Silence *(1962)*

such suggestion. We got around to talking about *The Magician*.

"It doesn't have anything to do with hypnotism, does it?" I asked him.

"No. No, of course not."

"Then it's a joke. A long, elaborate metaphor for the condition of the artist — I mean, any time, anywhere, all the time — "

He laughed in much the same conspiratorial way he had laughed when talking about his reasons for doing *The Seventh Seal*. "Well, yes. He is always on the very edge of disaster, he is always on the very edge of great things. Always. Isn't it

so? It is his element, like water is the element for the fish."

People had been interrupting us from the moment we sat down, and now someone arrived who clearly intended to take Bergman away with him. We made a date to meet early in the coming week. Bergman stood with me until my cab came and told the driver where I lived. I watched him, tall, bareheaded, and fearfully determined, as he walked away. I thought how there was something in the weird, mad, Northern Protestantism which reminded me of the visions of the black preachers of my childhood.

One of the movies which has made the most profound impression on Bergman is Victor Sjöström's *The Phantom Carriage*. It is based on a novel by Selma Lagerlöf which I have not read — and which, as a novel, I cannot imagine. But it makes great sense as a Northern fable; it has the atmosphere of a tale which has been handed down, for generations, from father to son. The premise of the movie is that whoever dies, in his sins, on New Year's Eve must drive Death's chariot throughout the coming year. The story that the movie tells is how a sinner — beautifully played by Sjöström himself — outwits Death. He outwits Death by virtue, virtue in the biblical, or, rather, in the New Testament sense: he outwits Death by opposing to this anonymous force his weak and ineradicable humanity.

Now this is, of course, precisely the story that Bergman is telling in *The Seventh Seal*. He has managed to utilize the old framework, the old saga, to speak of our condition in the world today and the way in which this loveless and ominous condition can be transcended. This ancient saga is part of his personal past and one of the keys to the people who produced him.

Since I had been so struck by what seemed to be our similarities, I amused myself, on the ride back into town, by projecting a movie, which, if I were a moviemaker, would occupy, among my own productions, the place *The Seventh Seal* holds among Bergman's. I did not have, to hold my films together, the Northern sagas; but I had the Southern music. From the African tom-toms, to Congo Square, to New Orleans, to Harlem — and finally, all the way to Stockholm, and the European sectors of African towns. My film would begin with slaves, boarding the good ship *Jesus*: a white ship, on a dark sea, with masters as white as the sails of their ships, and slaves as black as the ocean. There would be one intransigent slave, an eternal figure, destined to appear, and to be put to death in every generation. In the hold of the slave ship, he would be a witch-doctor or a chief or a prince or a singer; and he would die, be hurled into the ocean, for protecting a black woman. Who would bear his child, how

ever, and this child would lead a slave insurrection; and be hanged. During the Reconstruction, he would be murdered upon leaving Congress. He would be a returning soldier during the First World War, and be buried alive; and then, during the Depression, he would become a jazz musician, and go mad. Which would bring him up to our own day — what would his fate be now? What would I entitle this grim and vengeful fantasy? What would be happening, during all this time, to the descendants of the masters? It did not seem likely, after all, that I would ever be able to make of my past, on film, what Bergman had been able to make of his. In some ways, his past is easier to deal with: it was, at once, more remote and more present. Perhaps what divided the black Protestant from the white one was the nature of my still unwieldy, unaccepted bitterness. My hero, now, my tragic hero, would probably be a junkie — which, certainly, in one way, suggested the distance covered by America's dark generations. But it was in only one way, it was not the whole story; and it then occurred to me that my bitterness might be turned to good account if I should dare to envision the tragic hero for whom I was searching — as myself. All art is a kind of confession, more or less oblique. All artists, if they are to survive, are forced, at last, to tell the whole story, to vomit the anguish up. All of it, the literal and the fanciful. Bergman's authority seemed, then, to come from the fact that he was reconciled to this arduous, delicate, and disciplined self-exposure.

Bergman and his father had not got on well when Bergman was young.

"But how do you get along now?" I had asked him.

"Oh, now," he said, "we get along very well. I go to see him often."

I told him that I envied him. He smiled and said, "Oh, it is always like that — when such a battle is over, fathers and sons can be friends."

I did not say that such a reconciliation had probably a great deal to do with one's attitude toward one's past, and the uses to which one could put it. But I now began to feel as I saw my hotel glaring up out of the Stockholm gloom, that what was lacking in my movie was the American despair, the search, in our country, for authority. The blue-jeaned boys on the Stockholm streets were really imitations, so far; but the streets of my native city were filled with youngsters searching desperately for the limits which would tell them who they were, and create for them a challenge to which they could rise. What would a Bergman make of the American confusion? How would he handle a love story occurring in New York?

A FILMMAKER IN THE BORDERLAND:
BERGMAN AND CULTURAL TRADITIONS

MIKAEL TIMM

Mikael Timm is a cultural-affairs journalist, playwright, and film critic. This essay first appeared in the special tribute issue of the Swedish film magazine Chaplin, *titled* Ingmar Bergman at 70.

IN STUDYING THE EXTENSIVE LITERATURE ON INGMAR Bergman's films, you very quickly detect a difference compared with what is written about other directors. People who write about Bergman focus very much on the "message" of his films, while relatively few detailed studies have been devoted to his aesthetics.

The same pattern repeats itself if you look at press archives and study interviews with Bergman. Time after time interviewers and writers return to such themes as religion, love, morality, and the role of art in society. Like no other filmmaker, Bergman has been given the task of being a "moral" guide for his contemporaries. This is no marginal position, no mere concession to a new art form. On the contrary, Bergman has been awarded a number of prestigious "humanistic" honors otherwise bestowed on mainstream writers and scholars.

Personal interviews with Bergman present the image of a titanic artist in the romantic tradition, with Bergman the man more in the spotlight than his work. At the same time, his movies provoke lively debate. Some critics and viewers search for a "prophetic" dimension, containing truths about human society, the "ego," and the future. The filmmaker is assumed both to understand and to profess fundamental truths.

Personality cults are, of course, part of the cinematic tradition, but it is also unusual for new films to trigger serious debate. The seventh art was long regarded as an illegitimate form of culture. Whereas literary and art criticism has a tradition of painstaking studies, close readings, academic research, and self-evident participation in a broader humanistic debate, a long time passed before the cinema came close to achieving this role.

Even today, the difference between movie reviews and literary critiques in daily newspapers — at least in Sweden — is substantial, in terms of their level of ambition, the space allotted to them, and their frames of reference. And on television and radio, filmmakers are rarely asked the same kind of general questions about the spirit of their age that writers are somehow always expected to be able to answer.

Bergman is thus one of the few film directors

whose works encounter the same kind of expectations as do the more traditional arts and literature. Nevertheless, the cinema was barely considered an art form at the time Bergman began his first film projects. One only has to glance through the contemporary reviews of the films he made in the 1940s and 1950s to see how even those films that today are considered classics and a part of our common cultural heritage were treated as trivial entertainment.

Even after Bergman had made his international breakthrough, a Swedish textbook for journalists during the 1960s found it necessary to point out that "when writing a film review, remember to mention who directed the film, because the director is as important to a film as a writer is to a book." There are additional examples, which say something about the role of movies in the cultural marketplace.

Like no other form of art, the cinema stands at the meeting point between "polite culture" and a traveling minstrel show. Many serious students of the cinema regard this situation as awkward, if not embarrassing. But as the case of Bergman demonstrates, it may also result in an almost unique range and intensity of contacts between the artist and his audience. As a filmmaker Bergman is part of an industry devoted to producing and distributing entertainment. At the same time, his films have become increasingly important in our cultural life over the years.

In his capacity as a filmmaker, Bergman has experience of the different "cultural orbits" into which films can be placed. For many years, his films did poorly in commercial terms and his filmmaking could only continue because the Swedish motion-picture industry needed new products. Later his Swedish audience grew larger, while generally Sweden suffered declining film audiences. Bergman's salvation at that point was foreign audiences, which often encountered his works by way of film clubs, art movie houses, and the like.

Whereas Bergman's career as a filmmaker has been under threat on various occasions, he

A scene from Strindberg's A Dream Play *at the Royal Dramatic Theater of Sweden in 1986*

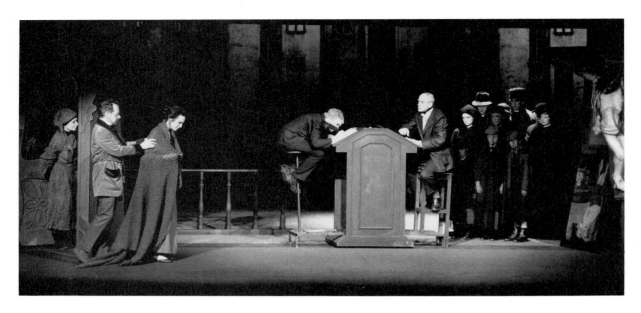

A scene from Strindberg's A Dream Play *at the Royal Dramatic Theater of Sweden in 1986*

has not only been tolerated by devotees of polite culture — of which the theater is one part — but also has been regarded as a theatrical director of extraordinary talent. He is, moreover, one of the most popular dramatists of his generation. Without viewing him from the standpoint of cinematic sociology, I believe that Bergman's distinctiveness and experimental nature derive much of their energy from the fact that he works in different aesthetic traditions and with different audience situations.

Bergman's cinematic production is commonly divided into phases: a first phase, in which he learned his craft and tried different means of expression; a second, in which he found his style — a "rose-colored" period — followed by a period of crisis, et cetera. This approach implies that there is an evolutionary process leading to a specific Bergman style, which can be defined and recognized.

This is a seductive line of reasoning and makes the role of the audience easier. But a quick look at Bergman's film production, with *Port of Call, The Seventh Seal, The Virgin Spring, Per-*

sona, Secrets of Women, From the Life of the Marionettes, Wild Strawberries, to mention just a few examples, instead proves the opposite. There is an incredible range of variations in Bergman's creations. Imagery, dramaturgy, conflicts, structure, the use of sound and music — all of these are different from film to film. During his long career, Bergman has never achieved one definitive style, but instead is continuously experimenting with new means of expression. He embraces and rejects themes, interpretations of characters, and narrative models — and returns to try them once more.

Bergman's last theatrical film, *Fanny and Alexander,* can serve as a gateway into his works. The film very quickly became such a popular, well-established concept that today the Swedes talk about "Fanny and Alexander decorations" in store display windows, "Fanny and Alexander celebrations" during the Christmas holidays, "Fanny and Alexander families," et cetera. For a Bergman work, the film was received with tremendous enthusiasm by an unusually large Swedish audience. Its drawing power was so great that the five-hour version did very well. It seemed as if the audience rather quickly reconciled itself with Bergman.

Fanny and Alexander transformed Bergman from a provocative filmmaker, whose greatest popular and critical successes of the preceding decade had occurred abroad, almost into a Swedish popular artist. The enthusiasm of the reception indicates that Bergman had previously been a provocateur of the first rank. What many people found appealing about *Fanny and Alexander* was the sense of harmony that characterizes the plot, especially in the five-hour version. All the conflicts are fully developed, the peripheral themes are interwoven elegantly and used to illuminate the main story; there is a powerful but seemingly effortless forward movement through the film. The dramaturgy, the linearity of the story, the set design, the actors' performances — everything fits together, in a way reminiscent of the great nineteenth-century novels.

Here are the forces of evil and good, men and women, childhood and aging, love and hate, individuals and groups, God and worldliness, faith and doubt, city and country, realism and dreams, water and fire. There are many pairs of opposites, but although the plot is fairly complex, with its entanglements and important side-intrigues, the story is constructed with almost inexorable stability. There may admittedly be shades of Griffith and Sjöström, but even clearer are the echoes of Dostoyevsky, Tolstoy, Thomas Mann, Dickens, and Balzac. *Fanny and Alexander* is of course a cinematic tale, but it is very firmly rooted in the major epic novel tradition.

As an individual film, *Fanny and Alexander* is a remarkable accomplishment. It appears even more remarkable if we look at Bergman's entire list of film credits. In the four preceding years, Bergman had made *From the Life of the Marionettes, The Fårö Document 1979,* and *Autumn Sonata*. It may seem almost incomprehensible that a single artist could work in such different genres with such good results. Although other filmmakers and, not least, film critics have often used the concept of the "Bergman film," it is difficult to see the kind of uniformity this phrase implies, either in terms of style or in choice of subject matter.

Sometimes Bergman's unique position in international cinema has been explained by the fact that he works with what might rather clumsily be called the "intimate sphere of the bourgeoisie." The idea here is that in numerous cultures, the bourgeoisie is similar and many moviegoers will therefore recognize what they see in Bergman's films. But this explanation is hardly sufficient, either to account for the exceptional response Bergman has elicited or to give his films any kind of unity.

The genres that Bergman works with are not unique to him: marriage dramas, historical films, contemporary psychological dramas, et cetera. Plenty of filmmakers have moved in the same cinematic landscape. Yet Ingmar Bergman has earned himself a special role in cultural life, unlike that of almost any other filmmaker. His films have been analyzed in terms of their ideas, morality, and ideology. Polite culture, which otherwise hardly admits movies into its world, has been very generous in Bergman's case. Why?

It is reasonable to seek the answer not in the themes or the aesthetics of his films, but in the tension between the ethical conflicts explored in these films and their aesthetic aspects. Such a reading emphasizes the breadth of Bergman's artistry rather than its uniformity, its dynamism rather than its clear-sighted stillness, its endeavors rather than its solutions. To me, Bergman's artistry is not of a kind that one can summarize and then file away. On the contrary, it is uneven and unfinished, and this is precisely what gives it a sense of urgency.

In Bergman's filmography, we can see a reflection of the entire cultural journey of the twentieth century. Of necessity, it is restless. It includes the great novelistic tradition, the work of early experimenters such as Meyerhold, modernism's dissolution of form and approach to time and space, naturalism, the eighteenth-century tradition of erotic wit, archetypal characters such as Faust, a Nordic tone in portraying the interplay

Lena Olin and Per Myrberg in Strindberg's A Dream Play *at the Royal Dramatic Theater of Sweden in 1986*

between man and nature, the alienation of the bourgeois family, and even some direct political references. In short, Bergman has based the creation of his films on the European cultural heritage before and outside cinematic art.

In his recent book *The Magic Lantern* (*Laterna Magica*) and in certain interviews, Bergman has told about his childhood and education. Although these events occurred only fifty or sixty years ago — when dadaism, symbolism, modern theater, industrialism, et cetera, were making their breakthroughs in Sweden — his origins are skewed more toward the social views and culture of the nineteenth century. It is a tradition where the writer served as a revealer of truths, where such Protestant concepts as guilt and responsibility were pivotal, and where it was farfetched to regard culture as a weapon or even as a force opposed to the stability of the bourgeois world. The works of art this culture created are in no way impoverished or simplistic. On the contrary, its heritage in the fields of prose, music, and the visual arts has turned out to be extremely vital. At the same time, this was the environment from which all of our twentieth-century attempts at cultural upheaval emanated.

The social opposite of this affluent Protestant milieu is, of course, the theater, which was hardly considered a defender of bourgeois ideals, despite the evolution it has gone through since the days of Molière and Shakespeare. When Ingmar Bergman began working in student theater, it was at a time of transition: the nineteenth-century tradition in acting styles, interpretation of works, and scenic design still survived on the major national stages, while at the same time modernism had made its breakthrough with full force and had already begun to establish its own traditions in other countries. Bergman's theatrical successes have sometimes been described as consisting mainly of unusual skill in instructing his players, but this is probably a simplification that leaves out most of the truth. On the contrary, many Bergman productions (I will choose examples from a small portion of Bergman's work) evidence a great familiarity with experimental theater. To take just a few examples: in *Woyzeck,* several productions of *A Dream Play,* and *King Lear,* Bergman's work utilizes drastic contrasts, simplifications, fast tempos, stylizations, et cetera. At the same time, he has directed productions of Shakespeare that neither hark back to the Elizabethan tradition nor base themselves on the institutional theater style that has its roots in the nineteenth century. As for his productions of the classics, one can speak of a respectful but not literal reading of the original texts.

In his theatrical productions, Bergman explores the same two traditions he does in his films. There has been a series of almost naturalistic productions (to take a recent example, Strindberg's *Miss Julie* in 1985), in which the director aims at the greatest possible degree of reality. On the other hand, there are productions such as *Woyzeck* (1968) and *A Dream Play* (1986) that are directly linked to twentieth-century experimental theater, abrupt, quick contrasts, daring set design, stylization, and brutal rhythm.

Obviously Bergman has used knowledge gleaned from his theater productions in his films, but, although this applies largely to his way of instructing the actors, there has also been a transfer of experience on another level. There are natural connections between modernism in the theater and experimental cinema. Even in Bergman's most daring films, where his narrative is most difficult to penetrate, it is clear that he has brought with him from the theater a respect for the rhythm of the actors in a particular scene and, not least, the realization that he must keep the audience with him. Some of his later films, such as *Autumn Sonata,* are sedately divided into "acts" and certain scenes open in a manner reminiscent of Ibsen.

By way of summary, in his theatrical work Bergman is even less faithful to any stylistic ideals than in his films: the range of playwrights — from Büchner to Ibsen to the dramas of classical antiquity — indicates that here, too, he can alternate between different traditions and dramatic styles. It becomes clear from his various Strindberg pro-

ductions that Bergman is capable of trying very different approaches to the same text. He does not arrive at a definitive interpretation of a play.

It is thus not possible to trace any mechanistic connection between Bergman's work in the theater and his filmmaking. As we know, it eventually became his routine to direct several theatrical productions each year, then with equal regularity use almost the same actors to make films during the summer. Obviously there is a connection, but it is more on the level of professional skills than of textual interpretation and aesthetics.

Having reached this point, it remains to be observed that the concept of a "European cultural heritage" is so general that it risks being unmanageable; it can encompass everything and at the same time be so vague in its contours that it becomes almost invisible. But the interesting thing about Bergman is that he does not assume a fixed position. In Bergman's work there is a continuous "rereading" of the classics and the aesthetic debate. At the same time, in his films he returns to the same moral themes, but only partly. Bergman's circle of motifs has expanded over the years.

The overall impression is that Bergman is constantly on the borderline between a harmonic approach to culture and a dissonant one. He is sufficiently skillful as a professional to succeed in holding together almost every film; the disunity of his vision is apparent only when you compare his films with each other.

It is not unique for a director to work at the point where different traditions intersect. On the other hand, it is unusual for him not to seek safety on one side of the border or the other, but instead to constantly alternate back and forth between them. Bergman does not accept with open arms the cultural heritage he receives. He is always thinking about rejecting it. There is a kinship of choice with other writers who worked in the same kind of borderland, such as Strindberg, Chekhov, and Pirandello.

Bergman has generally written his own screenplays. Most of his scripts have eventually been published. It was, admittedly, not Bergman's original intention that these scripts should be treated as literary works. The text is written in a coherent manner, yet, although his final films are often characterized by a strict and firm structure, his screenplays are "open." For example, they contain descriptions of smells and moods, which are not ordinarily found in a screenplay. Bergman's intention has been that these descriptions should inspire his various colleagues, set designers, and costume makers. But at the same time, these elements obviously make a Bergman screenplay resemble a lengthy short story or a short novel.

Without stretching the parallels too far, there are clear similarities with the prose of Chekhov and Turgenev. Bergman provides intimate descriptions and uses concrete details, from which the reader himself can construct the settings. There are elements of multileveled dialogue (sometimes small talk that floats past, sometimes confrontations), and an all-knowing narrator describes the state of mind of the main characters concisely and exactly, but without interpretations.

From Strindberg, Bergman borrows those techniques that are closest to the cinematic medium: precise details, lightning-fast changes of scenery, caustic dialogue, disruption of bourgeois harmony. It may seem a long way to Pirandello, but Bergman is Swedish in the same way that Pirandello is Sicilian: on an archaic, mythic level. Where Pirandello uses the sharp light, the smells, and the evident Catholicism of his landscape, Bergman uses Nordic mildness (sharp light stands for something frightening and evil in Bergman's films), the gray shades of his landscape, and its doubting Protestant pastors.

Many of Bergman's films are about writers, artists, and musicians, but above all he returns repeatedly to artists who inhabit the fringes of the artistic establishment: jesters, magicians, mystics. In a number of his films, Bergman travesties theatrical conventions, employing certain kinds of dialogue and humor and being faithful or unfaithful to a genre. His masterpiece here is *Smiles of a Summer Night,* which has very properly also been presented on the stage (with some difficulties) as *A Little Night Music.* Bergman chooses a discreet cinematic language. The editing of the film reinforces the dramaturgy, and the camera is used in a way that enables the actors to work with nuances that suddenly bring the genre alive. A rigid, ritualized drawing-room comedy gains a kind of intimacy through facial expressions, gestures, et cetera. All the people play roles and somehow realize their fates during a magic summer night. They are all standing on a stage.

Although a few writers, critics, or other scribblers pop up as characters in Bergman's works, the relationship between his films and literature is more complex and indirect than it is between his films and the theater. There are sometimes similarities in the narrative structure of prose works and films. This may apply both to the great European nineteenth-century novel and to experimental storytelling, as in his film *Persona.* On those occasions when Bergman uses a storyteller who turns directly to the audience, he sometimes does this to establish a kind of intimacy, as in a short story, and less often as a Brechtian distancing device. The artists, writers, musicians, actors, and jesters appearing in Bergman's films have in common that they very rarely find salvation and peace through their profession. It requires a moment of inattention on the part of fate if a jester is to escape demise and enjoy a little more of the good life.

It is generally fruitful to examine how Bergman uses dramatic climaxes and periods of rest, moments and continuities in his films. He combines his experience in the theater with both nineteenth-century epics and modernism in an eclectic fashion. In Bergman's hands, the cinematic medium is consistently a genuine fusion of art forms. The disunity in his script, for example, may find its counterpoint in his choice of film music. Bergman often contrasts a modernistic pictorial imagery with harmonic music. In other cases his imagery provides a frame of reference for other periods and works of art (the Middle Ages, Chekhov, the 1920s).

The epic structure of *Fanny and Alexander* is clear. In other cases the narrative has a fundamental pattern while the direction, rhythm, and acting diverge from the epic style and instead approach a dramatic one (for example, *Scenes from a Marriage*). His television series are interesting in this regard. In many ways, they resemble the nineteenth-century novel in terms of their actual production, their division into episodes, and the themes and characters that come and go. It is no coincidence that Bergman, who balances on the borderline between traditionalism and modernism, has become a significant innovator of the television medium, especially with his narrative series. TV drama itself seems destined to be forever stuck in nineteenth-century conventions, which are reproduced with state-of-the-art technology.

As for Bergman's relationship to the European cultural heritage, Swedes cannot close their eyes to the fact that people in other countries have often considered his films typically Swedish, not European. One reason Bergman's films have attracted so much attention outside Scandinavia is the "exotic" settings in which the stories take place. When Swedish movie buffs traveling abroad have been asked about Bergman's films, more than one has probably replied, "No, actually Sweden *doesn't* look like it does in Bergman's films." Most Swedes do not live in isolated houses in the countryside, most of them are not grappling with religious issues (or at least don't want to admit it), and, with the exception of some of his early films and the two TV series *Scenes from a Marriage* and *Face to Face,* most Swedes' manner of speech is different from that of Bergman's characters.

We know that films from a small remote culture have an exotic charm, yet audience reac-

Peter Stormare and Lena Olin in Strindberg's Miss Julie *at the Royal Dramatic Theater of Sweden in 1990, presented at the Brooklyn Academy of Music in 1991*

tions and reviews show that Bergman's works have an impact on people from other cultures in an apparently straightforward way. Bergman stands with both feet in the mainstream European cultural tradition, and this is a common platform for many people — regardless of what language they speak. It is also significant that a Japanese director such as Kurosawa, himself unusually Western in his education, feels a close kinship with Bergman's films. Like Shakespeare's England, Bergman's Sweden is a stage. Added to this is a more recent cultural heritage in which the landscape plays the part of the soul.

But if Bergman had merely contented himself with furthering a European cultural tradition — taking issues and character portrayals mainly from the nineteenth-century novel and putting them into a new art form — his films would have been not much more than workmanlike pieces. They would hardly have attracted such great attention and would not have earned him such a central position in cinematic history.

Bergman's decisive contribution is that, like all major artists, he has managed to renew not only his art form but also our way of viewing our own age. Just as all the early modernists had a well-defined bourgeois tradition as their starting point (Baudelaire, Appollinaire, Rimbaud, Duchamp, Weill, Brecht, Stravinsky, Picasso, and others).

Bergman's work presupposes both a clear tradition and the need to depart from it. He is both a symbolist and skeptical of his symbols. He does not rely on the results of his labor (it is striking how critical he is of both his films and theater productions). All he relies on is his working methods, his professional experience. His reexaminations employ the same tools that were used to build tradition.

In various contexts (most recently in *The Magic Lantern*), Bergman has stressed how important the theatrical tradition has been to him. From Torsten Hammarén and other stage directors he gained professional experience; they taught him the importance of thorough prepara-

tion, punctuality and discipline, respect for the actors' rhythm, and so on.

At a young age, Bergman became the head of a typical bourgeois cultural institution — a small provincial theater. Through all his crises and doubts, he has been faithful to institutional theaters. In the theater, the transfer of knowledge from one generation to another is a much more broad-based and living process than in literature and cinema, simply because a theater is a collective workplace that is in continuous operation.

With his roots in institutional theater, Bergman has been very much in the center of the clash between cultural heritage and innovation that has characterized twentieth-century aesthetics. When Bergman was a young director, there were still actors who worked completely in a nineteenth-century spirit. Meanwhile, the influence of Meyerhold and, later, Stanislavsky, Gombrowicz, Artaud, and many others was reaching the major institutional theaters in Sweden.

Although the cinema was long regarded as an illegitimate member of the cultural family — a role played today by video production — this young art form cultivated its own traditions all the more intensively. Young directors have always sat glued to their movie-house seats watching the works of previous generations again and again.

Sweden, too, has a silent-film tradition that must be considered unique compared with other art forms, and in many contexts Bergman has stated how he was influenced by Mauritz Stiller and Victor Sjöström. But, as I have indicated, there is nothing unusual about a film director studying the works of his predecessors very carefully. What is original about Bergman in this respect is not that he is closely related to Swedish or foreign cinematic traditions, but that he assumes that a film can be used to portray the same psychological processes as a novel.

A number of Bergman's films include the theme of the artist who is simultaneously drawn to the secure bourgeois life and rejects it. There is a bit of Thomas Mann's Tonio Kröger in several films. The more mature Bergman becomes as a filmmaker, the more caustically and inexorably he focuses on the destructive forces that flow beneath harmonic culture. Doubts and anxieties beset his characters. When war itself breaks out, there is no beauty — as is otherwise common in war films — but instead he shows naked and crude destructiveness, in the tradition of Büchner and von Sternberg.

What characterized Bergman's first period as a film director was his close adherence to existing genres. Unlike many young filmmakers of today who try to debut with radically different films, Bergman first tried to learn his craft. Later, after his cinematic artistry had matured, the influence of the theater was clear. The peak of this phase was *Smiles of a Summer Night,* which resembles a short story by Hjalmar Söderberg, Marivaux, or Lubitsch, but where theatricality — in the good sense — predominates.

In the 1960s Bergman entered a new phase: his films became increasingly experimental. This coincided with experiments in European theater and literature; Sartre and Camus were both dramatists and passionately interested in the cinema. Yet unlike Sweden's other great postwar film and theater director, Alf Sjöberg, Bergman rarely made any clear references to sources of intellectual inspiration or artistic isms imported from elsewhere.

Although many directors almost brag about how little they see of the works of contemporary filmmakers, throughout his career Bergman has carefully kept up with films. He has also devoted great attention to music and art. Despite the lack of references to aesthetic formulas, one can therefore assume that Bergman has been well aware of the debate over different aesthetic models, not least modernistic ones.

He himself has never presented a formula for how a good film or theater production should look. Instead, he has spoken in many contexts about the craft-related aspects of his profession, and about his respect for such knowledge. This respect has grown over the decades, but no corre-

sponding artistic model has emerged. He always continues his work by positioning each individual film and theater production at the spot in the aesthetic field where different forces and energy are at their greatest.

At the same time, his professional skill has continuously increased. The more he has mastered his means of expression, the more critical he has become toward his works. Instead of polishing his style, each film has served as a new contribution to his continuous test of "the potential of contemporary art." In other words: where should we stand on the scale between traditionalism and modernism?

On those occasions where Bergman has tried to be "topical" — to make clear references to a historical situation, as in *The Serpent's Egg* — this very quality has weakened his work. While other directors regard topicality as a source of energy that helps fuel their work, Bergman becomes bound by the limitations of the topical, because for him every individual film or theater production is a "project" where the creative process is replayed from the beginning.

Concretely, he can use his experience of actors working with conventional texts, where uniformity of interpretation is emphasized as a way of enhancing the power of modernism's fragmentary view of humanity. His experience of earlier productions makes him more familiar with the mechanics of the production process, but each time the results are unpredictable. He has a natural affinity with the high point of nineteenth-century tradition, just as it was approaching its own breakup and transition to modernism.

Bergman's latest theater productions, *King Lear* and *Hamlet* (in my opinion, the latter has been reviewed insensitively in Sweden), show his strong desire to experiment. In both productions, especially *Hamlet,* he stakes his whole reputation on the acting, challenging the text, the actors, and the audience instead of falling back on the kind of conventions that seem close at hand. This 1986 production of *Hamlet,* with its strong stylization, its provocative elements, and its almost brutal rhythm, might have been the work of a young director at the beginning of his career. Yet precisely because of his familiarity with traditions, Bergman can use every project to find a specific aesthetic language.

Bergman's works — that is, his individual films — have given powerful inspiration to artists in different genres, but because he straddles two traditions there has never been any "Bergman school" in theater or cinema.

In his constant desire to be ready to reexamine his achievements, to surrender the fort, and, after winning a battle, to be prepared to lose the next war, Bergman is ethically similar to such doubters as Dostoyevsky and Tolstoy and aesthetically to such modernists as John Coltrane, Stravinsky, Strindberg, and Picasso. Of course

not everything these men produced was good, but their art lives on. So will Bergman's. For although today's young directors cannot work in the same fashion in the borderland between the nineteenth and twentieth centuries, they have made similar aesthetic-strategic choices — to adopt a particular style, to develop a coherent aesthetics, or, like Bergman, to move between different positions and draw their strength from these constant changes themselves.

It seems unnecessary to add that Bergman's refusal to make definitive choices has been fruitful. It is necessary for the audience, like the seventy-year-old director himself, to risk everything on each new work. Bergman's work is not over, nor can it be over as long as one views his films with an open mind.

Translated by Victor Kayfetz

THE SIGNIFICANCE OF INGMAR BERGMAN

JÖRN DONNER

Jörn Donner has had a varied career as film director, producer, and author. Between 1978 and 1982 he was the managing director of the Swedish Film Institute, during which time he was executive producer of Fanny and Alexander. *He presently lives in Helsinki, Finland, where he has been active in politics.*

AROUND 1945 NEW TRENDS APPEARED IN ART, ALSO IN film. A change of generation was coming. The new names in Japan, Italy, and also Sweden had begun their work earlier. But the end of the war was a watershed, people say in retrospect.

Bergman made his first film as an independent director. Afterward people wanted to say that *Torment* is more his film than Alf Sjöberg's. Perhaps — for those to whom his later films offer the benefit of hindsight.

Bergman has often described how he felt when he made *Crisis*. He has probably somewhat exaggerated his total lack of professional knowledge. One result, in any event, was that over the years he became a craftsman and perfectionist. No aspect of working in films is unknown to him, they say. Later there were a lot of stories about how thorough he was and how he only rarely and reluctantly changed co-workers or actors.

In 1945 he was known in his native country as a theater director and writer. In Swedish literature it was a time of renewal. *Crisis* was no example of renewal. Yet, remarkably, there were critics who saw something new arriving with Bergman's first film. The fact that he of all people was allowed to make films was perhaps also related to the quantitative boom then prevailing, with about forty new Swedish films per year.

In the spring of 1949 I spent a week in Stockholm. It was my first trip abroad. In my youthful surroundings, people were talking about a film called *The Devil's Wanton*, which had just premiered. It was an upsetting experience for a sixteen-year-old to see this film, which seemed to open up whole new possibilities and left room for many interpretations. From that moment, Bergman became an artistic companion, sometimes a guiding star, stubbornness and frenzy personified.

The Devil's Wanton told in pictures what Swedish 1940s literature was saying in words. It was a time of artistic experimentation. *The Devil's Wanton* signified (we now know) the starting pistol of the Bergman epoch in Swedish cinema, the Bergman epoch in world cinema.

The Devil's Wanton was avant-garde. So was *The Naked Night*, at least judging by how diffi-

Max von Sydow with Bergman during filming of Hour
of the Wolf *(1966)*

cult it was for many critics to accept this relatively simple tale. *The Naked Night* is about an eternal theme, about love, jealousy, and degradation, but it is possible that something in its experimental form made the resistance great, just as it has always been when something new is being created.

Smiles of a Summer Night is definitely not avant-garde.

In a state of great personal difficulties, Bergman made this film, which received an award and much praise at Cannes, becoming the gateway to the external successes that followed, one after the other, until certain film critics, who had begun to tire of honoring the same gods, discovered that Bergman was passé and decided to honor other masters.

Henri Langlois of the Cinémathèque in Paris had discovered Bergman before *Smiles of a Summer Night*. Bergman was one of many minor names in Paris, a city which had functioned for many years as the intellectual clearinghouse of world cinema. Then and much later, Langlois showed series of Bergman films, and made the young French generation aware of Bergman's qualities — something that made Truffaut have his young hero steal a still photo from *Monika*, a token of his respect for Bergman.

From that period in the 1950s, the success of Bergman's films spread like rings on water. They became standard fare for those exclusive Parisian movie houses that constantly make it possible to revive past years and old films.

Bergman became a business phenomenon. This could not have happened with production conditions under which studios aimed at high profits and a world audience. It was only possible under conditions where they were accustomed to short filming periods and unpretentious fees. The world audience materialized, was found in many countries, especially France and the United States, but it was not large, compared with what the Bond films of a later period required.

Bergman the business phenomenon, and his international reputation, made it possible for the Swedish government — after a one-man campaign by Harry Schein — to agree to a film re-

form in 1963 that was financially unique, securing the economic position of Swedish cinema for years to come.

Bergman the business phenomenon gave Bergman the artist freedom that was limited, to be sure, but within the limits he was able to be true to himself. So he created such ascetic and distant films as *Winter Light* — also underestimated for almost as long as *The Naked Night*.

The auteur concept was coined in France and presupposed that one could compare the work of a film director with that of a writer. Cinematic images thus became as personal as poetry or prose. Behind the technical gadgetry, a single person was concealed.

Based on this philosophy, the most peculiar personalities were born — for example, certain professionally able directors who had worked in Hollywood for years and had never filmed their own screenplays, instead operating mainly within the framework of an entirely commercial system. But among them — and this was perhaps the discovery — several had a personal signature.

According to this conception, the overshadowing Nordic auteur was Bergman — almost a godfather to the movement, without having to be regarded as guilty of its critical excesses.

At the same time, this meant that in Sweden his role was perceived as negative by many, among them Bo Widerberg. If there was going to be a revolt against the Swedish cinema as it was, it had to be aimed against Bergman.

This was perhaps partly because he had a strong position when it came to production decisions. Somewhere along the line, it must have occurred to him to function as a godfather-sponsor-producer for the new Swedish cinema, building up a community of young artists who learned from his experience and know-how.

Actually this combination fit him badly, because by definition his path to success could not be imitated, at least judging from what I tried to say in an early book about Bergman (1962) — that his career as a filmmaker was unique, that it

Bergman, Ulf Johanson, and Liv Ullmann during the filming of Face to Face *(1975)*

was built on altogether specific experiences and knowledge which could not be imitated.

In retrospect, the idea that Bergman the producer would create a bunch of little plastic-Bergman auteurs seems absurd.

He realized his failure in this respect at an early juncture. Then he made one of his many necessary departures, this time to the theater. No one else could make films the way Bergman himself did, because everyone's handwriting is unique.

What is Ingmar Bergman trying to say?
This question was being asked in more and more countries from Australia to the United States to Sweden. Critical persons said he didn't

have anything at all to say, that he was actually creating intellectual puzzles without answers, while the philosophically or religiously schooled published long, grave essays or books about him.

The world of the 1960s in a larger number of Western countries was definitely not postwar in spirit, and there was a not entirely unfounded optimism about the future. There was also a larger number of people for whom existential problems were more important than social or economic ones. Most of Bergman's films have lacked explicit social messages.

Of the many references to "Bergman's landscape," his visions and individual images, I remember an automobile journey in one of V. S. Naipaul's novels. After the fact, when I now check how the text reads, the female partner in the story merely says: Bergman.

That says everything, or nothing.

It was possible to travel around the world and talk about Bergman, because he was a topic of conversation. But much later (1981), when I was trying to persuade the Chinese that *Autumn Sonata* was a remarkable film, they said they preferred *The Brothers Lionhart,* because "such" problems as those in *Autumn Sonata* "did not exist" in China.

On the other hand, they apparently existed in the Soviet Union, because Soviet intellectuals — probably illegally — had seen a large proportion of Bergman's films, and he *was* a topic of conversation there.

Even after he has ended his film career, he will remain a topic of conversation.

Someday, and I really hope it is a distant day, a psychologically knowledgeable and biographically schooled researcher is going to compare Bergman's nightmares and dreams (in his films) with the reality he has lived through, and discover that his films are actually an endless, cleverly masked autobiography, in the same way that his official autobiography, *The Magic Lantern,* is cleverly masked.

There are numerous hints.

Bergman himself has told about how he finds visions and material from dreams and daydreams. It means he is childlike, that he combines a child's curiosity with a child's wisdom and naïveté. That childishness has enabled him to overcome the natural inhibitions and limitations of actors. They have been able to rely on him the way children rely on someone (to the extent they do).

Childishness also means an ability to summarize a course of events in a single, simple symbolism. Childishness is the ability to unmask.

One then wonders, as the researcher should do, is it the screenplay, the directing, the actors? If not, what? I don't know if Bergman's scripts should be classified in literature as dramas or novels. They bring to the films a material rich in associations. Some of them are so meager that an outsider could hardly have made pictures from them. The sensuality and mood that the pictures convey, the series of images that return with a new content, could be conveyed through film and no other medium.

This unparalleled childishness continued through nearly forty years of cinematic history. It has no parallel and cannot be linked with any other well-known name. Truffaut is perhaps closest, however. But he is a disciple.

A superbly stupid but (objectively speaking) relatively harmless string of events made Bergman — via Paris and Los Angeles — eventually settle in Munich. He eventually obtained his redress but did not move home until he considered the time ripe and he had reconquered Sweden through theater directing and *Fanny and Alexander.*

Some years earlier I had met in Paris with Joseph Losey, an emigrant from the United States (for the sake of his convictions) and driven out of Britain (for the sake of taxes). He took exile such as he and Bergman suffered as the most natural of things.

Bergman, however, wanted to get revenge on Sweden, and he devoted more space to this in his autobiography than it deserves.

But this, too, was important, considering that Bergman has been inner-directed, little controlled by outside impulses. In his pedantry and careful guarding of his own freedom and his working discipline, this incident came to signify a lot, because until then he had been entirely his own master. Now an outsider had wanted to control his physical freedom.

In the long run, Bergman would probably be unthinkable other than as a Swede. How Sweden reacted to what he did was always important. In many films there are triumphant victories or degrading defeats. Everything ends in a certain ironic reconciliation. This also happens in *Fanny and Alexander,* which is an anthology (in the best sense of the word) of Bergman themes, and therefore perhaps misunderstood.

The path to self-understanding is difficult. Bergman's private self-understanding is one thing; it does not concern us here. Artistic self-understanding leads a person to try to make a synthesis of the chaotic and irrational conditions of private life and external life, which is often dissimulation and playacting.

Bergman's films have a defiant spirit that makes his moral significance even greater than his strictly artistic significance. And that is important. Others have written about all the rest.

Translated by Victor Kayfetz

Bergman's Trilogy: Tradition and Innovation

ROGER W. OLIVER

> Nothing changes more constantly than the past; for the past that influences our lives does not consist of what actually happened, but of what men believe happened.
>
> — Gerald White Johnson

> The past is the present, isn't it? It's the future, too. We all try to lie out of that but life won't let us.
>
> — Eugene O'Neill, *Long Day's Journey into Night*

THE INESCAPABLE INFLUENCE OF THE PAST ON THE PRESENT is probably the keynote to naturalism as a literary/dramatic theory. Since heredity and history are two of the determining factors of naturalism (along with environment), the actions of the characters in naturalistic plays are inevitably shaped by the past. For a director staging the works of such playwrights as Ibsen, Strindberg, and O'Neill today, the challenge is not only to convince a modern audience of the acceptability of such a deterministic philosophy, but also to avoid the tyranny of the past imposed by more than a century of naturalistic productions.

While Ingmar Bergman's productions of *Miss Julie, Long Day's Journey into Night,* and *A Doll's House* may not have been initially conceived as a naturalistic trilogy, they functioned as such when viewed in this order, the order in which Bergman directed them and the Brooklyn Academy of Music presented them, in 1991, as part of the second New York International Festival of the Arts. Each production clearly delineated the themes and conflicts of the individual play in and for itself; taken together, however, the three stagings illustrated not only the kinship between the three plays thematically and stylistically, but also Bergman's evolving approach to reconciling traditional and contemporary theatrical practices.

Although Ingmar Bergman has been associated with the Royal Dramatic Theater of Sweden (Dramaten) since 1960, these three productions represent some of his work with the company since his return from his self-imposed exile in Germany. The oldest of the three productions, *Miss Julie,* was first presented in Stockholm in 1985 and is based on a production he first staged in Munich. In certain ways it is the most "traditional" of the three stagings, retaining the kind of meticulously detailed *mise-en-scène* usually associated with plays of this type. Yet even within the context of a "realistic" presentation of the play, Bergman is able to make discoveries about the work that illuminate and enliven it for a contemporary audience.

The close connection between tradition and innovation in Bergman's work can perhaps best be illustrated by the physical appearance of Miss Julie herself. When German playwright Peter Weiss was consulting the original manuscript of the play in preparing his text for Bergman's Munich production, he discovered a reference to a scar Miss Julie bears on her face from a whipping by her fiancé. Weiss and Bergman decided to restore the scar, which Strindberg himself had deleted, since it visually establishes Julie's vulnerability and provides further motivation for the fear and loathing of men she exhibits during the course of the play. According to Gunilla Palmstierna-Weiss, who designed all three of the Bergman productions seen at BAM, Bergman connects this scar with the one Julie receives as a result of her loss of virginity during the Midsummer Eve interlude and her anticipated use of the razor provided by Jean at the play's end. Julie's victimization at the hands of the men in her life thus encompasses not only the neglect by her weak father but also the physical abuse by her fiancé, and the seduction and then betrayal by Jean.

Perhaps the most effective demonstration of Bergman's ability to use realistic detail to create the world of the play onstage occurs in the Midsummer interlude. While Jean and Julie are offstage in Jean's bedroom, Strindberg calls for the following scenario:

> Led by the fiddler, the peasants enter in festive attire with flowers in their hats. They put a barrel of beer and a keg of spirits, garlanded with leaves, on the table, fetch glasses, and begin to carouse. The scene becomes a ballet. They form a ring and dance and sing and mime: "Out of the wood two women came." Finally they go out, still singing.

For Bergman the scene becomes less a festive folk ballet and more a richly detailed exchange between individualized figures who party, drink, and explicitly express their sexual desires. Since some of the peasants have entered the kitchen previously, looking for water, there is a sense of continuity within the life of the household as well as the play itself. Strindberg's dramatic device for eliminating an intermission and allowing sufficient time for a significant action to occur offstage has been heightened by Bergman into a variant of the passions being expressed by the central characters offstage. Even though the peasant couples are not given dialogue, their body language, gestures, and actions clearly convey the reality of Midsummer Eve.

This reality is underscored by Bergman's casting and conceptualization of the role of Kristin, the cook who rules over the kitchen and is also Jean's fiancée. Kristin is often cast so that her stolidity and plainness contrast with Julie's neurasthenic vibrancy. By choosing an attractive young actress, Gerthi Kulle, to play Kristin, and directing her to explicitly express her sensuality, Bergman emphasizes her needs and helps motivate the tenacity she exhibits in fighting Julie for Jean. When Kristin is left alone in the kitchen, for example, instead of curling her hair, as indicated in Strindberg's stage directions, in Kulle's performance she washes her upper body, including her breasts, slowly and sensuously, simultaneously expressing her need to refresh herself after working in a hot kitchen, and her awareness and appreciation of her own physicality.

In all three Bergman productions seen at BAM, in fact, it was the physical relationships of the characters as they interacted with each other and their environment that communicated the director's vision of the plays. For example, the way in which Peter Stormare, as Jean, opened the bottle of wine, smelled the cork, poured some into a glass, and then tasted it perfectly expressed the character's peculiar amalgam of aristocratic hauteur and servility. The brutal way in which he threw Lena Olin's Julie to the floor underscored the antagonism as well as the attraction he felt toward her. According to several members of the Dramaten, Bergman stages his productions very meticulously, providing the actors with specific movement patterns as well as physical actions.

Bergman's willingness to adjust his production to fit the individual actor, however, is illustrated by a crucial change in costume for Miss Julie. The working kitchen that Palmstierna-Weiss has provided for this production is in various shades of gray, on which Hans Åkesson's lighting can create stunning effects marking the passage of time and change of mood. When Bergman first created this production for the Dramaten, the actress playing the title role — Marie Göranzon — wore a lavender dress that fit in with the color scheme of the room and suggested a sense of belonging, despite her status as the mistress of the house. For the performances at BAM, where Lena Olin assumed the role of Miss Julie, a red dress was substituted, reinforcing the passionate intensity and fierce individuality the new actress brought to the role. In this version, when Miss Julie changes out of her red dress into her traveling costume in anticipation of her departure with Jean, her loss of control is underscored by the fact that she no longer dominates the stage visually the way she did previously. In certain ways this production is the apotheosis of naturalism, with each physical and visual detail made as telling as possible to contribute to the vitality and verisimilitude of the whole.

With his production of *Long Day's Journey into Night* we see Bergman moving toward a more abstract approach to naturalism. Instead of the minutely specific setting she created for *Miss Julie*, Palmstierna-Weiss has ignored O'Neill's stage directions for a reconstruction of his parents' Monte Cristo cottage. The play's action takes place on a platform set within a void. In addition to a few chairs, the room is furnished only with a religious statue on a pedestal on one side and a liquor cabinet on the other. Occasionally, projected images, like the exterior of the house or a large tree, appear on the rear wall; otherwise, the action unfolds on a sparsely furnished platform surrounded by black curtains.

Bergman's approach to O'Neill's text also invites us to view the play in a new way. (This is perhaps the time to note that the Dramaten gave the world premiere performances of *Long Day's Journey into Night,* in 1956, with Jarl Kulle, the

Bibi Andersson and Thommy Berggren in Eugene O'Neill's Long Day's Journey into Night *at the Royal Dramatic Theater of Sweden in 1988, presented at the Brooklyn Academy of Music in 1991*

Pernilla August and Per Mattsson in Ibsen's A Doll's House *at the Royal Dramatic Theater of Sweden in 1989, presented at the Brooklyn Academy of Music in 1991*

actor presently playing the father, James Tyrone, in the role of Edmund.) Unlike most productions, where there are two intermissions or one intermission between Acts II and III, the Bergman version pauses after the third act, thus making the daytime and early-evening action continuous and isolating the final midnight scene. Substantial dialogue is cut throughout the first three acts, including all of Edmund's story about the pig farmer and the oil tycoon that O'Neill later dramatized in Act I of *A Moon for the Misbegotten*.

The main effect of this theatrical structure is to place the emphasis on Mary Tyrone in the first part and the three Tyrone men in the second. There is no question that Mary is the focal point in the first three acts of O'Neill's text. But by presenting these three acts as a unit, Bergman

underscores her descent into a drug-induced fog to escape her fears over Edmund's illness. Bibi Andersson's unforgettable portrayal of Mary stresses the physical and emotional pain the character suffers, graphically depicting the agonized despair created by her alienation from family, friends, her past, and even her own body. All four actors portraying the Tyrones (in addition to Kulle and Andersson, Thommy Berggren as Jamie and Stormare as Edmund) perfectly capture the complex love-hate relationships of the play and the alternating rhythms of infliction of pain followed by the search for forgiveness.

By emphasizing the split between the part of the play dominated by Mary and the final scene, in which the men try to understand and gain pardon from each other, Bergman allows his audience to become more aware of the kinship between *Long Day's Journey into Night*, *Miss Julie*, and *A Doll's House*. Like the earlier playwrights, O'Neill is exploring the complexity of the male/female relationship and its dependence, not only on inherited distinctions of gender but also on social roles and conventions that are part of the individual and collective history of the characters. Mary, like Nora, has gone from her father's house to her husband's, though she complains that James has never really given her a proper home.

To stress the difference between the world of the first three acts — Mary's world — and that of the final act — the men's domain, Bergman and Palmstierna-Weiss shift our perspective for Act IV. In his stage directions O'Neill calls for one living-room setting throughout, informing us that at the rear are two double doorways with portières, one of which "opens on a dark, windowless back parlor, never used except as a passage from living room to dining room." By substituting a different set of chairs for the ones used in the first three acts and turning the statue and liquor cabinet around, we see that the men, like wounded animals, have retreated into their lair to lick their wounds after Mary has once again failed to kick her addiction.

In this final act, moreover, Bergman brilliantly ties his visual and structural approaches to the play together. Peter Stormare has been quoted as saying that instead of doing *Long Day's Journey into Night* as a realistic play, Bergman "wanted to do it more like a dream that becomes a revelation in the night." It is through Stormare's portrayal of Edmund that Bergman achieves this sense of dream/revelation. When Edmund speaks to his father about his experiences at sea, instead of speaking extemporaneously, he reads from a notebook. Edmund has already begun to transmute his life into art. At the play's end, when Mary intrudes into the men's drunken world dragging her wedding gown (in this production accompanied by the maid, Catherine, whom she has awakened), the characters do not all remain onstage in the dazed tableau suggested by

O'Neill. James and Jamie accompany Catherine as she attends to Mary, and Edmund remains onstage alone. He then takes out his notebook and begins to write. The "play of old sorrow" as O'Neill himself called *Long Day's Journey into Night* has both ended and just begun.

Bergman's version of *A Doll's House* both continues and extends the movement toward abstraction and textual distillation found in his production of the O'Neill masterpiece. Once again the design is dominated by an island-like platform that is sparsely furnished. Here there is a greater sense of containment, however, as high walls extend the entire height of the sides and rear of the stage. While there is seemingly more of a nod toward realistic detail in the presentation of the Helmer home, the black-and-white photographic blowups used for this purpose also serve to emphasize Bergman's lack of interest in naturalistic illusion.

This denial of theatrical verisimilitude is reinforced by the chairs on either side of the acting platform. Here the actors who are not on stage in a particular scene sit in full view of the audience. When they are to appear in a scene, they make a swift, immediate entry, not only accelerating the pace of the action, but underscoring the ways in which the lives of these characters are tightly interwoven.

One of the great achievements of this production is the extent to which Bergman has liberated *A Doll's House* from its well-made-play baggage. Although reinforced by the production, it is in the text he has helped fashion from Ibsen's original that this accomplishment chiefly lies. By eliminating completely the peripheral figures of the nurse, housemaid, and porter, and reducing the number of the Helmer children from three to one (a daughter, Hilde), Bergman concentrates the focus even more tightly on Nora and her relationships with Torvald, Dr. Rank, Krogstad, and Mrs. Linde. He then goes even further by downplaying the resolution of the actions involving the latter three characters, so that we are really concerned only with Nora and Torvald in

Pernilla August in A Doll's House *at the Royal Dramatic Theater of Sweden in 1989, presented at the Brooklyn Academy of Music in 1991*

Act III. Thus only Mrs. Linde comes to the Helmers' house at the beginning of the act, and there is no card from Dr. Rank in the mailbox announcing his imminent death.

By this third production in his "naturalistic trilogy" Bergman is willing to intervene more drastically into a play's structure so that he can rid it of melodramatic effects and make the characters' actions more plausible. He not only cuts substantial material from the early part of the act but also restructures the latter part so that Act III is played in two scenes rather than one. The first scene concludes in the middle of the Nora-Torvald confrontation, after he learns that Krogstad will not expose Nora's actions. Rather than thank Nora for her love and sacrifice in borrowing the money that helped save his life, Torvald offers to forgive her, acknowledging that he will have to be even more protective of her in the future.

Instead of an immediate segue into Nora's announcement that she is leaving Torvald and her family, the curtain falls. When it rises on the second scene, several hours have passed. Torvald is in bed, naked except for the sheet covering him. We are to infer that he and Nora have slept together, perhaps in one last attempt on her part to see if there is anything that can keep them together. Torvald's words, "Why, what's this? Not in bed? You've changed your clothes," thus take on a much greater significance. As Nora reveals her epiphany to Torvald, he is not only naked, defenseless against her accusations and analysis, but also immobilized, lest he offend decorum. When Nora makes her exit, through the audience, she has separated herself from him unequivocally. The sound of the slammed door reinforces the finality of her action. By separating the scene into two parts, with the suggested time passage in between, Bergman has allowed his Nora to come to a conclusion that is well thought out and therefore more convincing.

The care with which Bergman builds to this final scene is evident throughout the production. From her first entrance Pernilla Östergren's Nora has suggested the character's strength and determination. She plays the submissive and fluttery role that society and her husband demand of her, but without sacrificing her inner sense of self-worth. When she realizes that she is totally confused by the mixed signals the men in her world have sent her, she decides she must strike out on her own. How can she teach her daughter how to behave in this society when she doesn't know herself?

Balanced against Östergren's strengthened Nora is Per Mattsson's Torvald: less the priggish male chauvinist and more the prisoner of values he has inherited and unquestioningly accepted. Stripped of the trappings of the well-made play, *A Doll's House* is more clearly a play about people threatened by old values and the behavior they generate. Nora and Torvald also come to seem the victims of their materialist society. With his promotion at the bank, the Helmers have finally "made it" and Torvald is terrified of anything that might threaten his position and authority. Bergman's production thus highlights the connections Ibsen makes between patriarchy, materialism, and suppression.

Taken together, then, these productions reveal a double progression, thematic and theatrical. Thematically Bergman is examining these plays as three alternative examples of male-female conflict within a materialist society. In *Miss Julie* sexual antagonism reinforced by class differences results in death. In *Long Day's Journey into Night* the dependency caused by traditional gender roles leads to drugs and despair. It is only when an individual like Nora is willing to make the courageous (and antisocial) act of leaving material comfort and security behind that freedom and self-knowledge is even remotely possible, though by no means a certainty.

Just as Nora is forced to view the past in a fresh way during the course of Ibsen's play, so Bergman forces us to look at these plays anew, both individually and in relation to each other. He accomplishes this by progressively stripping them of the naturalistic theatrical trappings that might have been necessary when first produced but now may obscure more than clarify. With *A Doll's House,* the earliest and the most familiar of the three, Bergman must take the most radical approach, both textually and theatrically, so that the essence of the play can be revealed. Like an expert stripping a painting of layers of accretions so that the original underneath can be revealed, Bergman and the artists of the Dramaten enable a contemporary audience to see these plays not as theatrical relics but as vibrant contributions to our ongoing dialogue on gender, power, wealth, and class.

BERGMAN AS NOVELIST

CARYN JAMES

Caryn James is a film critic for the New York Times. *She has also been an editor of the* New York Times Book Review.

"FROM AN EARLY AGE ONWARD," INGMAR BERGMAN writes about himself, "it was said that 'Ingmar has no sense of humor.'" He writes this in a deadpan manner many comedians would envy, by way of explaining why, in 1951, he happily directed commercials for a soap called Breeze. "They rescued me from a severe financial setback," he says of the television spots, adding that they "were made in good spirits. One can even overlook the fact that they promoted a soap that practically tore the skin off your body." Ah, the unknown Bergman. He is everywhere in *Images: My Life in Film,* a series of wry, lucid, often harsh reflections on his life's work that was published in Sweden in 1990 but did not appear in English translation until 1994.

Images is not the most recent of Mr. Bergman's books to appear here, and it is certainly not the last word on the little Ingmar, "considered sullen and too sensitive." It is not easy to keep up with his literary output since he stopped directing feature films in 1982.

Sunday's Children, an exquisite autobiographical film about his boyhood, was written by Mr. Bergman and directed by his then twenty-nine-year-old son, Daniel. And Ingmar Bergman's novel of *Sunday's Children* has just been published as well. In the hands of most former filmmakers, the novel might be a watered-down version of the movie. But *Sunday's Children* is as elegant, honest, and emotionally brutal as *Fanny and Alexander;* though its scope is slender, this brief novel is a perfectly shaped treasure that stands among the finest work of Mr. Bergman's career.

The freshness of *Sunday's Children* in both its forms is amazing, because Mr. Bergman has written this story before. It exists nearly whole, in subject and shape, in the next-to-last chapter of *The Magic Lantern* (1987), the first of the autobiographical books that have made Mr. Bergman, now seventy-six, one of the most alluring writers of recent years.

In *The Magic Lantern,* one July the young Ingmar accompanies his father, Erik, from their country house to a nearby village where Erik Bergman, a minister, is to preach. Ingmar is a Sunday's child, according to folklore, able to see fairies and other visions. He takes the trip with his father by ferry and bicycle, and recalls seeing in

Bergman and Erland Josephson as Isak Jacobi relaxing on the set of Fanny and Alexander *(1981/82)*

the church a stained-glass window depicting "Death leading a dance to the Dark Lands, wielding his scythe like a flag" — a picture that would become the final scene of *The Seventh Seal* and one of the most famous Bergman images of all. Comically, Ingmar's older brother, Dag, promises to pay him for eating a live worm, then reneges on the offer after the boy with the notoriously fussy stomach has swallowed the creature. These are major incidents in *Sunday's Children*, too.

More striking, that chapter in *The Magic Lantern* includes flashes forward in time to the adult Ingmar Bergman visiting his elderly, widowed father. Their relationship is one of fear, anger, coldness. In expanded form, those forward flashes become the harsh emotional underside of

the lyrically beautiful *Sunday's Children*, on screen and on the page.

"I am forever living in my childhood," Mr. Bergman writes in *Images*. As the details of those July days echo from memory through *The Magic Lantern* on to *Sunday's Children*, they hold the key to the art of Mr. Bergman's memoirs. He keeps returning to his past, reassessing it, distilling its meaning, offering it to his audience in dazzling new shapes.

In *Sunday's Children*, the young Ingmar is an eight-year-old called Pu (on screen played by the golden-haired, wide-eyed Henrik Linnros). He is a serious child who both loves and hates his father and is already troubled by the idea of death. When film and novel flash ahead to 1968, the fifty-year-old Ingmar is still angry and intransigent on his visits to Erik. In a dizzying swirl of connections between father and son, the middle-aged Ingmar is played on screen by Per Myrberg, who looks nothing like the real Mr. Bergman. But his father is played by Thommy Berggren, who as he ages looks quite a bit like Ingmar Bergman today.

Judging the adult Ingmar harshly, Mr. Bergman has made *Sunday's Children* a huge gesture of reconciliation to his now-dead father. It is also a great gift to his son. (It is easy to speculate that Mr. Bergman's ramshackle personal life, with eight children spread among four wives and one lover, might make such gestures especially prized.) Daniel Bergman made children's films and worked for television before filming *Sunday's Children,* his first feature. When the project was conceived, father and son agreed that Ingmar would write without consulting his son, and Daniel would direct without his father's help. Ingmar Bergman stayed away from the set of *Sunday's Children.*

The importance of the screenplay is suggested by the vast difference between *The Best Intentions,* the rich, trenchant 1991 film about his parents that was written by Ingmar Bergman and directed by Bille August, and the sprawling fiasco of *The House of the Spirits,* written and directed by Mr. August. Only the luxurious scenery in those two films is similar.

In *Sunday's Children,* too, capturing the graceful, picturesque quality of two days in the country is the easy part. Daniel Bergman's cinematographer, Tony Forsberg, even substituted for Sven Nykvist on *Fanny and Alexander* for a few weeks when Mr. Nykvist had the flu.

But Daniel Bergman has done more than create a pretty film that echoes his father's lyricism. Daniel and his actors capture the tormented emotions beneath the picturesque summer in the country. Pu is a darling, sympathetic little boy. "Shut your mouth, Pu," his Uncle Carl says. "You look stupid with your mouth open." The comment is repeated by Pu's nanny and by Dag, but you have to return to *The Magic Lantern* to discover why Pu's mouth is always gaping. Adenoid problems caused the young Ingmar to breathe through his mouth, "which made me look stupid," Mr. Bergman writes.

Pu is also preternaturally serious, like the famously humorless little Ingmar. Both film and novel rely on his relentless questions. Pu keeps asking "What?" like a nervous tic. When a servant tells a ghost story about a local watchmaker who hanged himself, the tale becomes a fantastic set piece on the page and an eerie black-and-white vision on screen. The watchmaker kills a demonic grandfather clock and a small, fully formed woman who lives inside it. Later, Pu goes to the place where the watchmaker killed himself and asks in a dream, "When will I die?" The watchmaker answers, "Always," an idea that the filmmaker has carried with him throughout his career.

Similar though the two versions of *Sunday's Children* are, each makes a unique contribution to the grand mosaic of the Bergman biography. On screen, the adult Ingmar's coldness is more visceral; in the novel, the connections between past and present are stronger and more resonant.

When Pu sits on the edge of the ferry and dangles his feet in the water, his father swats him on the head in fury, which leads directly to a flash forward. "What did I do wrong?" the aged father asks, having discovered his dead wife's diaries, which call their marriage "a life-fiasco." The adult Ingmar coldly, even cruelly, tells his father how frightened the family was of his anger. Then he walks away. The scene returns to Pu and his father, who apologizes for pulling the child away from his dangerous perch on the ferry so violently. "I was scared," he says. "When you're scared, you get angry." The explanation goes back to *The Magic Lantern* and to the heart of the Bergman family's anger and unhappiness. Pu, having overheard his parents arguing, fears that his father will leave; Erik fears losing his wife; over the years, Ingmar's anger becomes implacable.

Mr. Bergman deftly positions his leaps in time to reflect backward and forward, so the pres-

Bergman rehearsing Bertil Guve (Alexander) during filming of Fanny and Alexander *(1981/82)*

ent illuminates the past and the past explains the present. On screen, when the camera returns from 1968 to Pu's boyhood, the flashes forward almost seem to have been prophetic visions of this Sunday's child. On the page, the effect is the opposite, as the voice of Ingmar Bergman today is heard shaping his past.

On their way home from the sermon, Pu and his father are caught in a storm. The father puts his coat around Pu, and the story jumps ahead to Erik Bergman's deathbed. Erik whispers a blessing on his son, who is unable to understand what his father is mumbling. As the story returns to the past, Erik once more puts his coat around Pu, echoing the gesture of blessing. *Sunday's Children* itself is a blessing that Ingmar Bergman has bestowed on Daniel. This son had the good sense and talent to appreciate the gift and turn it into an enduring Bergman film.

THE IMAGINED PAST IN INGMAR BERGMAN'S
THE BEST INTENTIONS

ROCHELLE WRIGHT

Rochelle Wright is Associate Professor of Scandinavian, Comparative Literature, and Cinema Studies at the University of Illinois at Urbana-Champaign, where she has taught since 1975. She has published extensively on twentieth-century Swedish fiction and translated two novels by the Swedish writer Ivar Lo-Johansson. She is currently writing a book on the images of ethnic outsiders in Scandinavian film.

Near the beginning of *Bilder* (1990; *Images,* 1994), his recent retrospective commentary on his films, Ingmar Bergman reveals the autobiographical underpinnings of *Smultronstället* (1957; *Wild Strawberries*):

> I tried to put myself in my father's place and sought explanations for the bitter quarrels with my mother. I was quite sure I had been an unwanted child, growing out of a cold womb, one whose birth resulted in a crisis both physical and psychological. (17, 20)[1]

The penultimate scene of the film, where Sara leads Isak Borg to a sunlit bay across which he can glimpse his parents, is characterized as "a desperate attempt to justify myself to mythologically oversized parents who have turned away, an attempt that was doomed to failure" (22). Bergman further states that only many years later was he able to establish contact with his parents as fellow human beings and thus achieve some measure of reconciliation and understanding.

In the final chapter of his autobiography, *Lat-erna Magica* (1987; *The Magic Lantern,* 1988), Bergman describes how, after listening to Bach's Christmas Oratorio in Hedvig Eleonora Church, he imagines stepping into his former home across the street and thereby into the past. He encounters his mother, Karin, who has been dead for many years, writing in her diary, and bombards her with questions about family relationships:

> Why did I live with a never-healing infected sore that went right through my body? . . . I have no wish to hand out blame. I'm no debt collector. I just want to know why our misery was so terrible behind that brittle social prestige. (284–85)

An arsenal of possible explanations and motivations does nothing to reduce Bergman's sensation that "I hurtle headlong through the abyss of life" (285). In this dream, his mother does not respond

Bergman with the children in the cast of Fanny and Alexander *(1981/82)*

directly to his insistent questioning, she merely deflects it; she is too tired; he should talk to someone else. Then her image dissolves. Back in the present time of the narrative, Bergman recalls that her diaries, found after her death, revealed a woman whose innermost thoughts no one in the family had known.

Examining old photographs in chronological sequence, as he did in the short film *Karins ansikte* (1986; *Karin's Face*), had allowed Bergman to construct a visual narrative about his mother, but he recognizes that he has not gained access to her inner reality or traced behavior patterns to an ultimate source. In *The Magic Lantern* he posits a partial explanation for his inherited burden of unhappiness and repression: "[O]ur family were people of good will but with a disastrous heritage of guilty consciences and too great demands made on them" (289). The autobiographical volume ends with a quotation from his mother's diary, written only a few days after his own birth, that exposes her ambivalence both about her marriage and about her infant son.

Taken together, these passages from *Images* and *The Magic Lantern* suggest Bergman's reasons for writing *Den goda viljan* (1991; *The Best Intentions,* 1993), a fictional account of his parents' early years together, from 1909 until 1918. (In the original Swedish, the title of the last work alludes directly to the lines from *The Magic Lantern* quoted above; the phrase *god vilja* may be rendered either 'good will' or 'best intentions' in English.) *Wild Strawberries* is hardly the only Bergman film to explore the parent-child relationship. The importance of his own childhood experiences to his development as an artist has been abundantly attested, both by Bergman himself and by critics. In *The Best Intentions,* however, he attempts to see his parents from another point of view, not as the mythical giants who dominated his childhood, but as complex individuals whose conflicts and struggles were not primarily focused on him. By concluding the narrative in 1918, the year he was born, he avoids the possible distortion of his own memories, in which he himself is the protagonist. He strives for

a perspective that in one sense is objective because it is not self-serving, but that nevertheless relies on intuition and empathy. His investigation may also, albeit indirectly, offer him some insight into himself. "Why should I otherwise take so much trouble?" (105), he asks rhetorically.

Bergman's text is properly considered primarily in the context of a Swedish tradition of autobiographical and historical fiction; it is quite separate from the six-hour, four-part television series of the same title, directed by Denmark's Bille August, which first aired in Sweden in December 1991. Bergman knew when he wrote *The Best Intentions* that he would not direct it. Though he states in the prologue that he envisioned Pernilla Östergren (now Pernilla August) and Samuel Froler as his parents — they were indeed cast in those roles — he granted Bille August complete freedom to make whatever changes and cuts he desired in the manuscript, and he was not involved in the filming process. The published text, in turn, has not been altered to conform to the television series, which itself underwent further transformation. Pared to less than half its original length, a feature-length version of *The Best Intentions* was submitted in competition at the 1992 Cannes Film Festival, where it won the Palme d'Or and Pernilla August received the award for Best Actress.

The book is thus a separate entity, distinct from any filmed version, even more than is usually the case with a Bergman screenplay; Bergman himself notes in the prologue that he provides much information that cannot possibly be translated into a visual medium, though it may serve to help the actors in their interpretations. In fact, the text is a prose narrative with stretches of dialogue rather than a conventional screenplay. Most of this narrative is composed in the third person, but Bergman also breaks in periodically to speak in what presumably is his own voice, offering comments and interpretations, a feature that is completely absent from the television series and film. This self-reflexive attitude toward the process of creation and the ongoing analysis of the narrator's role in the selection and presentation of ma-

Bergman orchestrating the dinner party of Fanny and Alexander *(1981/82)*

terial are an integral part of the narrative and establish *The Best Intentions* as a metanovel where much of the discussion explicitly revolves around the reliability of the account and its basis or lack thereof in documentary reality. The following observations will focus exclusively on Bergman's text.

In his prologue to *The Best Intentions*, Bergman emphasizes its fictional component: "I have drawn on my imagination, added, subtracted, and transposed, but as is often the case with this sort of game, the game has probably become clearer than reality" (i). Later, the text is referred to as "the story or the action or the saga or whatever" (107), and the author periodically reiterates that "this is no chronicle, requiring a strict accounting for reality. It's not even a document. . . .

I possess fragmentary notes, brief tales, isolated episodes" (105). The most detailed explanation of Bergman's attitude toward the historical past comes almost exactly in the middle of the narrative:

This account turns arbitrary, main issues into subsidiary issues and vice versa. Sometimes it indulges in huge digressions in the tradition of oral storytelling. Sometimes it wishes to fantasize over fragments that appear out of the dim waters of time. Unreliability on facts, dates, names, and situations is total. That is intentional and logical. The search takes obscure routes. This is neither an open nor a concealed trial of people reduced to silence. Their life in this particular story is illusory, perhaps a semblance of life, but nevertheless more distinct than their actual lives. On the other hand, this story can never describe their innermost truths. It has only its own momentary truth. (135)

The mere fact that Bergman has not felt constrained by his (admittedly limited) knowledge of actual events comes as no surprise to anyone familiar with the allusive and indirect way he has incorporated his own memories and experiences in previous works. What is illuminating, in *The Best Intentions* as in his entire oeuvre, is the artistic purpose of these transformations, the internal dynamics governing his artistic reconstruction of the past.

The Best Intentions gives an intimate psychological portrait of its protagonists in an effort to show how, despite their love for each other, despite the best of intentions, their relationship does not lead to happiness for either of them. Bergman's starting point is a conception of character, an interpretation of his parents' personalities that derives from various sources: to some degree from documentation and specific conversations with them about the early years of their marriage, but also from his own personal knowledge of them in later life, from understanding achieved after their deaths, and, most important, from his own imagination and intuition. He has made little attempt to piece together a verifiable sequence of events. Though he claims to have read his mother's diary, he seems to have mined it for psychological insight rather than factual information. The narrative he constructs offers a plausible, but not factual, version of their lives that neither justifies nor condemns, but, rather, explains and illustrates. It is an imagined past, a sort of alternative universe, that only partly overlaps with the past of historical record.

A comparison between events and chronology in *The Best Intentions* and the actual experiences of Bergman's parents, Karin Åkerblom and Erik Bergman, is possible through an examination of the record they themselves left behind. After the death of both parents, Bergman and his siblings agreed that their private papers would remain in the possession of the youngest child, Margareta. In 1992, only a few months after *The Best Intentions* appeared, a selection of these documents was published, with additional biographical information and commentary provided by the editor, Birgit Linton-Malmfors, under the title *Den dubbla verkligheten. Karin och Erik Bergman i dagböcker och brev 1907–1936 (A Double Reality. Diaries and Letters of Karin and Erik Bergman, 1907–1936)*. Included are excerpts from Karin's private diary, from a family chronicle that she also prepared, from an autobiography composed by Erik for Margareta in 1941 (though she was instructed not to read it until after his death), and from letters, the majority from Erik to Karin or from Karin to other family members, in particular her mother. (Karin seems to have destroyed most of her letters to Erik.) Though the documentary record as presented here is far from complete, it suffices to establish a reliable outline of the period covered in *The Best Intentions*. There is no reason to suspect the editor of deliberately distorting the facts or of attempting to manipulate the view of Karin and Erik Bergman that the documents convey.

A detailed, point-by-point examination conclusively demonstrates that the fictional narrative and the various factual accounts differ profoundly, even more so than Bergman's own interpolated commentary indicates. By discussing several specific discrepancies, I will suggest some general principles according to which Bergman recasts and reinvents his material.

The character of Henrik, based on Bergman's father, Erik, is established early in the narrative, which opens with his refusing his paternal grandfather's request that he be reconciled with his grandmother on her deathbed (a rebuff that calls to mind Bergman's own rejection of a similar request from his mother when his father was hospitalized and very ill). In the second scene, Henrik fails an important examination in church history and is unable to find solace from his fiancée, Frida. A visit to his anxious, overprotective mother, who constantly refers to the sacrifices she has made on his behalf, only increases his guilt. Their scheme to borrow more money from three rich maiden aunts by deceiving them about his academic success is humiliating and nearly backfires. Henrik's pride and self-assertiveness are revealed as a façade designed to hide his insecurity, lack of self-esteem, and separation from meaningful human contact.

In contrast, Anna, drawn on Bergman's mother, Karin, is secure in her position as the much-loved only daughter in a large, close-knit, economically privileged family. She is charming and intelligent, but spoiled, headstrong, and accustomed to getting her own way. The couple meets when Anna's brother Ernst, a friend of Henrik's and a fellow student, invites him to dinner at their home. It is Anna who takes the initiative in their relationship, and it is she who fights back with determination when her mother opposes it.

The Best Intentions emphasizes not only the psychological dissimilarities between the protagonists, but also the social and economic disparity in their situations. In actuality, Bergman's parents were second cousins and met when his father paid a duty call on the Åkerblom family at the time he began studying at Uppsala; Ernst was thirteen years old at the time. The maiden aunts who finance Henrik's education in *The Best Intentions* had their correspondents in real life, but they were relatives of Bergman's mother as well, and it may have been at their estate that his parents first got to know each other well. There is no mention of kinship between the protagonists in the fictional narrative, since such a connection would be contrary to Bergman's decision to highlight contrasts and differences.

A Double Reality documents the opposition of Karin's mother to her choice of husband, though little specific information is offered. The battle of wills between mother and daughter becomes a major theme in *The Best Intentions*, where the mother intervenes at two crucial junctures: first, by using her knowledge of the engagement to Frida to blackmail Henrik into breaking off with Anna, and, much later, by intercepting and burning a letter from Anna to Henrik in which she reaches out to reestablish their bond. In the fictional narrative, the couple is separated for two years; not only does Anna refuse all contact with Henrik during this time, but she also becomes ill with tuberculosis and goes abroad to receive care at a sanatorium, and then embarks on a tour of Italy with her mother. Her father's death during their absence prompts her mother to confess to having burned the letter to Henrik against the wishes of her husband. Upon returning to Sweden Anna seeks out Henrik and they begin planning their life together.

The actual progress of the relationship between Bergman's parents was far less dramatic. Though their courtship was not without difficult moments, there is no evidence of any cessation of contact, and the frequent physical separations came about because Karin was training as a nurse in Göteborg and Stockholm while Erik continued his studies in Uppsala. Karin did become ill, but her time abroad consisted of an eighteen-week trip taken with her mother and brother. Her father lived until 1919, after Bergman was born.

These examples should suffice to illustrate how Bergman departs from historical fact in order to create tension and drama. The interpretation of his parents' characters and personalities appears to be consistent with the documentary evidence, but many, if not most, of the events described in *The Best Intentions* are fictional, the product of Bergman's imagination. Sometimes Bergman explicitly states that this is the case, for instance with regard to the episode he presents as a turning point in the relationship between Anna and Henrik, an explosive quarrel in the chapel near their future home. This scene is an extrapolation, an imagined scenario, one of many possible scenarios.

> It's always hard to trace the real reason for any conflict. . . . One can imagine quite a number of alternatives, both random and fundamental. Go ahead, you can browse and speculate: this is a party game. (175)

Gunnar Björnstrand as Filip Landahl in Fanny and Alexander *(1981/82)*

If we construe Bergman's exhortation to "go ahead" as being addressed to the reader as well as himself, it follows that we are included in the author's imaginative game: we are encouraged to question his interpretation of the argument's significance or to envision another version of events entirely. In her essay "The Director as Writer: Some Observations on Ingmar Bergman's *Den goda viljan*," Louise Vinge points out that Bergman's technique of introducing the reader into his creative process is characteristic of a postmodern work.[2] He sets the stage, but the performance continues in our mind's eye.[3] Bergman thus relinquishes control of his own artistic production.

In a fictional account, obviously, Bergman is free to alter facts to suit his own purposes and to position the reader not only as spectator but as codirector. There the matter would rest, were it not that he periodically calls attention to the documentary sources of the narrative, sometimes in a manner that seems designed to create confusion about what is historical fact and what is not. The names of the characters are a case in point. The protagonists of *The Best Intentions* are called Anna and Henrik, but early in the narrative Bergman punctures this fictional disguise. After a long descriptive passage, he sums up as follows:

> That's what she looks like — Anna, my mother, whose name was really Karin. I neither want to nor am able to explain why I have this need to mix up and change names: my father's name was Erik, and my maternal grandmother's was Anna. Oh, well, perhaps it's all part of the game — and a game it is. (18)

Bergman's comment implies that Anna and Henrik both are and are not fictional characters, and both are and are not to be identified with Bergman's own parents. That the fictional narrative switches the names of real-life mother and grandmother — Karin becomes Anna, Anna becomes Karin — at first seems perversely designed merely to create confusion, but it also suggests that in Bergman's imagination, their identities

Bergman with longtime cinematographer Sven Nyk-vist

merge. The choice of the name Henrik for a prickly, self-involved, romantic young man tormented by self-doubt should be familiar to students of Bergman's early films. It is interesting that in his subsequent autobiographical narrative, *Söndagsbarn* (1992; *Sunday's Children,* 1994), in which his eight-year-old alter ego plays a central role, Bergman calls his parents by their actual names. Though this novel is also a fictional reconstruction, it draws in part on Bergman's own personal memories rather than his recollection of others' versions of the past, as was the case in *The Best Intentions.* Perhaps his own participation in the action of the narrative and his consequent (relative) lack of distance to the material led him to more closely identify the fictional characters with their real-life counterparts.[4]

The deliberate blurring of the boundaries between fact and fiction established by Bergman's "name game" plays an important role throughout *The Best Intentions.* For instance, the text states, "My parents were married on Friday, March fifteenth, 1913" (184). Clearly, Bergman can marry off the fictional characters Anna and Henrik on whatever day he pleases, but the text appears to refer to Bergman's real-life parents, Karin and Erik, since we assume the first-person narrator to be Bergman himself. The actual wedding date of the elder Bergmans was Sept. 19, 1913; March 15 was the day their engagement was formalized. A slip, a memory lapse? This explanation cannot account for the fact that Bergman (or, rather, strictly speaking, the first-person narrator) notes that though no wedding picture has survived, he has before him a wedding invitation — which, one assumes, would state the date on which the nuptials were solemnized. Either Bergman is referring to an imaginary document — a possibility that is not as fanciful as it may seem at first — or he chooses, for reasons known only to him, to mislead the reader deliberately. Perhaps by blurring the distinctions between the fictional Anna and Henrik and the historical Karin and Erik, Bergman is suggesting that our perceptions of others, our responses to them, and our interpretations of their behavior ultimately are based on imagined constructs that we ourselves impose. As Louise Vinge states, "Illusion and reality seem to have fused in the author's mind through the creative work" (292).

In other instances, too, it is difficult to establish whether Bergman is referring to actual documents, letters, and photographs, or whether these objects should be construed as belonging exclusively to the fictional narrative. Letters attributed to Anna or Henrik in *The Best Intentions* appear to have been composed by Bergman rather than excerpted from authentic letters exchanged between his parents, and are presented as part of the imagined universe. References to photographs and visual images, however, are often ambivalent or deceptive. When Bergman begins a passage with the words "The picture [or image] shows . . ." it cannot always be determined whether he is describing a photograph, real or imagined, or imagining the completed film, or both. A particularly complex example of this confusion occurs in *The Best Intentions* with regard to a portrait of the Åkerbloms taken while Henrik is visiting the family. Bergman assures the reader that this photograph actually exists, an impression he reinforces by meticulous specification of what it depicts and by mention of examining it through a magnifying glass. At the same time he casts doubt on its authenticity by stating that though the photograph probably dates from 1912, he places it in 1909 in the fictional narrative because "it fits better into this context" (76). He describes Henrik and Ernst as both wearing student caps in the photograph and states that it is "quite clear" that

Henrik is present in the capacity of friend of Ernst rather than suitor of Anna. This strains credulity when applied to the real-life situation, for Ernst had not taken his matriculation examinations in 1912, let alone 1909, and furthermore was eight years younger than Bergman's father. But Bergman continues:

> Go into the photograph and recreate the following seconds and minutes! Go into the photograph as you want to so badly! Why you want to so badly is hard to make out. Maybe it's to provide some somewhat tardy redress to that gangling young man at Ernst's side. (77)

The phrase "Go into the photograph" may be read in several different ways. If one posits the existence of an actual photograph, this invitation or command may simply be Bergman giving himself permission or urging himself to imagine and describe the circumstances under which it was taken. This interpretation is supported by Bergman's explanation in the prologue to *The Best Intentions* that he inherited a number of photograph albums after the death of his parents and that these images fascinated him. More generally, however, "going into" the picture may be construed as a metaphor for the visual imagination. The reference in the quotation to "the following seconds and minutes" may allude to Bergman's chosen medium of film, in which still images are connected in a narrative sequence in time, and more specifically to the film of *The Best Intentions* that he imagines or envisions. The prologue further states:

> I go into the photographs and touch the people in them, the ones I remember and the ones I know nothing about. It is almost more fun than old silent films that have lost their explanatory texts. I invent patterns of my own. (i)

In *The Best Intentions,* Bergman demonstrates that the imagined past has its own validity, coherence, and autonomy, whatever its documentary basis. In fact, since the actual historical past can never be fully reconstructed, the imagined past is all that is left — to him, and to us.

Notes

[1] Here and elsewhere, page references are to the published English translations of Bergman's works, though I have studied them in the original Swedish.

[2] *A Century of Swedish Narrative*, 286.

[3] *Ibid.,* 285. Vinge analyzes the ambiguous way Bergman uses the Swedish word *föreställning,* which may refer both to the imagination and to stage performance, and offers an enlightening interpretation of how the quarrel scene comments on "the relation between illusionary art and reality" (291) in Bergman's text.

[4] Bergman's greater personal involvement with the subject matter of the second novel is also suggested by his selection of his own son Daniel, rather than an outsider, to direct the subsequent film.

Works Cited

Ingmar Bergman. *The Best Intentions.* Trans. Joan Tate. New York: Arcade Publishing, 1993.
—— . *Bilder.* Stockholm: Norstedts, 1990.
—— . *Den goda viljan.* Stockholm: Norstedts, 1991.
—— . *Images: My Life in Film.* Trans. Marianne Ruuth. New York: Arcade Publishing, 1992.
—— . *Laterna magica.* Stockholm: Norstedts, 1987.
—— . *The Magic Lantern: An Autobiography.* Trans. Joan Tate. New York: Penguin Books, 1988.
—— . *Sunday's Children.* Trans. Joan Tate. New York: Arcade Publishing, 1994.
—— . *Söndagsbarn.* Stockholm: Norstedts, 1993.
Birgit Linton-Malmfors, ed. *Den dubbla verkligheten. Karin och Erik Bergman i dagböcker och brev 1907–1936.* Stockholm: Carlssons, 1992.
Louise Vinge. "The Director as Writer: Some Observations on Ingmar Bergman's *Den goda viljan,"* in *A Century of Swedish Narrative: Essays in Honour of Karin Petherick.* Ed. Sarah Death and Helena Forsås-Scott. Norwich, U.K.: Norvik Press, 1994.

The Typically Swedish in Ingmar Bergman

MAARET KOSKINEN

Maaret Koskinen is a professor of film history and criticism at the University of Stockholm. She is the author of a study of Bergman's film aesthetics and is currently researching a book on the relationship between his film and theater work. In the spring of 1994 she was a visiting professor at Cornell University.

When we imagine hell, we extend the worst we already have. Most of us in the Western world would envisage social chaos. Who but a Swede would have a nightmare of body and mind totally irreconcilable, projected into a milieu dwindled to fewer than a dozen people who can't talk to each other, with the sun setting at 2 p.m.?

— Vernon Young[1]

THIS DESCRIPTION OF INGMAR BERGMAN'S *THE SILENCE* (1962) can be said to summarize the often clichéd conception of what is "typically Bergmanian": a Lutheran, not to say Puritan, streak ("body and mind totally irreconcilable"); isolation and lack of communication between people ("people who can't talk to each other"); and general gloominess ("the sun setting at 2 p.m."). However, Young considers these ingredients to be not only "typically Bergmanian" but apparently also "typically Swedish." Who if not a Swede, he asks rhetorically, would make a movie like *The Silence?*

Young sets out from an implied assumption, namely that the correlation between Bergman's world and the world we call reality — in this case the Swedish reality — is in some way "positive," direct, and unproblematic. *Wild Strawberries,* for example, is seen as depicting Sweden's "favorite misery":

In every country, to be sure, there are people who have abdicated from life, "the world forgetting and by the world forgot." But in no other country to my knowledge are there so many people who have turned their backs on society while remaining in it. This ancient ruin, Mrs. Borg, deserted by her son and ignored by her grandsons, this undoting father who has made loans to his son at exorbitant rates of interest, and the son, declaring to his wife, "My need is to be dead. Absolutely, totally dead," are all *familiar Swedish phenomena* [my italics]. So, at the end, Isak Borg is sentenced to loneliness. . . . To no

Swede would isolation be a capital punishment. *Ensamhet: loneliness.* Their favorite misery. They cherish it; they hug it to themselves, they write odes to it . . . [170].

It cannot be expressed more clearly than this: *Wild Strawberries* (1957) is a kind of spiritual documentary about Sweden and the Swedes' perverted yearning for loneliness.

The fact that a naïve, one-dimensional comparison like this between the "Bergmanian" and the "Swedish," between fiction and reality, flourishes in more popular contexts is perhaps not so surprising. The cinema is thought of as a mirror with a near-mystical ability to reflect reality "as is," or as a window to the world, a transparent, art-less window where — as in Magritte's famous painting — there is no ontological boundary between the reproduction and the represented. The cinema is regarded as a substitute for reality, instead of as a parallel, an addition.

This approach to cinema is probably due to its "built-in" realism. For one thing, it reproduces objects photographically, and, even more than a realistic novel or painting, it conveys the impression — the illusion — of "capturing" the world and reality; and, for another, it is a medium of moving pictures, which further enhances this illusion. But this is, of course, no excuse for treating cinema as if its very nature or essence lies in this illusion, in this purely photographic resemblance to reality.

The representation and the represented are different phenomena. As we know, a copy is not the same as the original, a map not the same as the territory. A picture — even a moving picture — is never reducible to its original; on the contrary, it is always something *beyond,* something more than the tangible object that it depicts. Film is a language, not a "reality"; it is distinction, not resemblance. As with all other arts, film gives reality a meaning it does not intrinsically have. This distinction between cinema as language and as representation must consequently serve as the starting point if we want to compare Bergman's films and Swedish reality.

One critic who understands this distinction

A classic scene from Cries and Whispers *(1971)*

is Jörn Donner, in his book on Ingmar Bergman.[2] Donner bases his analysis on the transformation of Swedish society during the past forty years, a period when Christian norms and solidarity have increasingly yielded to more secular norms. But since these new norms did not succeed in filling the void and replacing the old norms, a spiritual unrest emerged in Swedish society. One symptom of this unrest, according to Donner, is Bergman's films, which are all — even the most idyllic ones — characterized by a sense of crisis (see page 11). The Christian element in Bergman's films becomes not a direct expression of "Swedish" religiousness but a paradoxical sign of the lack of religiousness. It expresses less a presence than an absence: the void that "has remained" after material welfare has been taken care of. Or, as Bergman himself is supposed to have said, "When all the problems seem to be solved, then the difficulties come."[3]

The Lutheran Christianity in Bergman's films thus becomes a paradoxical expression of the fact that Sweden is one of the most secularized countries in the world, something that most Swedes don't give a thought to. In the eyes of foreign interpreters, Bergman's films seem at their most Swedish precisely when they are at their most un-Swedish!

Swedish Nature — and Girls

Constantly trying to prove a connection between Bergman's movies on the one hand and a supposed Swedish reality on the other hand is not only extremely problematic but also quite limiting. The danger is that people will use the films as a kind of Rorschach test in order to express an opinion about something else, about something "Swedish" outside of the films.

In searching for the specifically Swedish in Bergman's films, it is thus relevant to place them in their own sphere: Swedish culture and its traditions. This is especially relevant given the fact that there are probably few film directors so thoroughly rooted in their own country's artistic tra-

ditions as Bergman is (which he is the first to admit).

Bergman has especially strong ties with Swedish silent film. As Leif Furhammar has pointed out, his roots in the past are stronger than his own influence on the younger generation of Swedish directors.[4]

Perhaps the most characteristic feature of Swedish silent films — which made them world-famous — was that they brought nature into the dramatic action. (Remember that at that time it was still relatively unusual to film outdoors and even more unusual to take artistic advantage of the setting.)

Victor Sjöström's *Terje Vigen* (1917) and *The Outlaw and His Wife* (1918; also known as *You and I*), for example, are famous for their magnificent images of nature and for the way they created an interaction between man and nature. Equally renowned is Mauritz Stiller's *Sir Arne's Treasure* (1919),[5] based on a story by Nobel Prize–winning novelist Selma Lagerlöf, especially the scene in which the women trek across the ice in a snowstorm, carrying the dead heroine.

A similar feeling for the moods and interaction between man and nature is perhaps especially evident in Bergman's early films, in which the Swedish summer plays a prominent part. The titles themselves reveal this: *Illicit Interlude* (1950), *Summer with Monika* (1952; U.S. title *Monika*), *Smiles of a Summer Night* (1955).

In these early films the summer landscape tends to be either a realistic background to the action or, as foreground, the object of lyrical descriptions of nature. In either case, nature has great intrinsic value and exists largely for its own sake. Or in critic Marianne Höök's graphic words:

> . . . summer is the main character, the inviting semi-dusk of the summer night, the glittering water, the shadow of a boat across the bottom, a fishing rod in a rowboat, the peacocks dragging their vanity between the trees in the white nocturnal light. . . .[6]

Just as during the silent-movie period, this Berg-manian feeling for nature was interpreted — especially abroad — as very Swedish, even exotic.

In this context, keep in mind that Bergman's early movies were released around the same time as the worldwide triumph of Arne Mattsson's *One Summer of Happiness* (1951), which was furnished with similar stage decor: the bright Swedish summer night and, of course, Swedish girls, i.e. Swedish "sin." The fact is that Bergman's "stage decor" attracted particular attention from the critics.

> There is something about Swedish girls like Ingrid Thulin and Bibi Andersson, something that goes straight to the heart of all men; they have some kind of mystical chemical attraction which withstands every analytical effort.[7]

This British (and most likely male) reviewer was obviously so enchanted that he almost declared himself bankrupt as a critic!

Also indicative of this attitude were the titles chosen in the United States for Bergman's movies, even those that had nothing to do with summer and "sin." The film known in Britain as *Waiting Women* (1952) became the mysteriously enticing *Secrets of Women;* the innocent *Summer Games* (1950), the original Swedish title, became *Summer Interlude* in the U.K., only to evolve into the sinful *Illicit Interlude* in America. Even the fairly complex film known in Britain as *Sawdust and Tinsel* (1953) became *The Naked Night* in the United States.

The Dream of Summer

The sensuous beauty of Swedish summer nature and of the summer girls in Bergman's movies of the fifties has great intrinsic value. But just as in the Swedish silent films, these images of nature are charged with meanings that go beyond their documentary status. An example of this is in *Monika,* which is about two young people spend-ing the summer in the archipelago outside Stockholm. The plot follows the changes in nature. With its glittering water, its space and light, the archipelago in summer becomes a dream of happiness and freedom. When the couple returns to the city and reality, not only the summer but also their love is over.

A similar contrast is found in *Illicit Interlude,* but here Bergman's imagery takes on greater weight through the roles of time and memory. The story is told using a flashback technique and is about a young woman, Marie, and her development from a young girl into a maturing artist. The memory sequences, which describe summers Marie spent with a student, Henrik, are dominated by space and light, as in *Monika.* The scenes from the present are consistently gloomy and confined: dark city streets, an autumn storm tearing through naked branches, rain beating down. In other words, the passage of time and the changes that accompany it are depicted through changes in nature: Youth stands against aging, innocence against experience, play against seriousness; summer becomes the foremost sign of a past, of a time relentlessly gone. It becomes the very image of a paradise lost.

Characteristically, *Illicit Interlude* includes, for the first time, something that became a recurrent symbol of a summer paradise in Bergman's films. When Marie first meets Henrik, she takes him to her secret wild-strawberry patch. There they crawl around on all fours like children in a presexual Eden.

Bergman returns to the wild strawberries in the famous sequence of *The Seventh Seal* (1956) in which Mia offers wild strawberries with milk to the Knight: "I shall carry this memory between my hands as if it were a bowl filled to the brim with fresh milk," he solemnly says. For one precious moment he has escaped the struggle with his silent god and has found a paradise on earth.

The next year strawberries found their way into the very title of a Bergman film: *Wild Strawberries.* As in *Illicit Interlude,* the inner world of the main character is shown through the mecha-

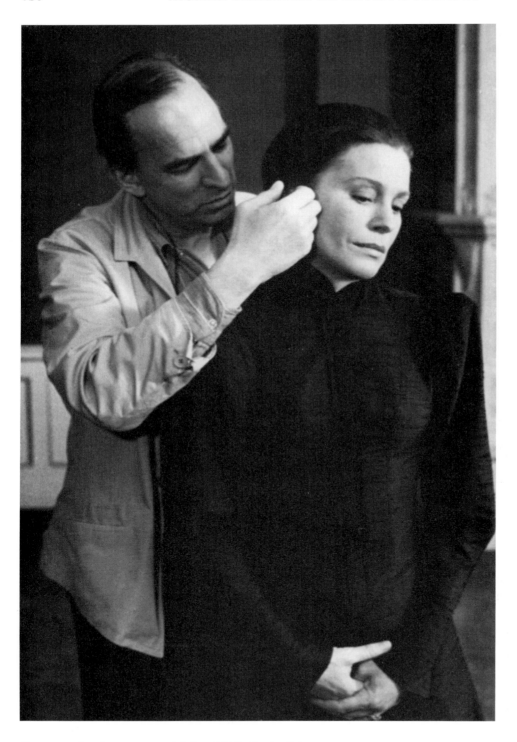

Bergman shaping a scene with Ingrid Thulin in Cries
and Whispers *(1971)*

nism of flashbacks, and again wild strawberries are associated with memories and dreams and with a lost paradise where everything is drenched in white summer light. In the words of the main character, Isak Borg: "The clear reality of the day faded into the even clearer images of memory, which rose before my eye with the strength of a real event."

In the film's last dream sequence, the old professor sees himself sitting in the wild-strawberry patch with his first love, Sara. "No more wild strawberries," she says sadly, and above them the clouds gather. When there are no more wild strawberries left, the clear light of summer, too, disappears. But then she leads him through a dark forest, and suddenly in front of him is an inlet with water smooth as glass. On a sunlit peninsula on the other side, his parents, dressed in white, sit and wave at him. And so the movie ends, with a close-up of the blissful face of the professor: He has finally found peace, found his way back to his wild-strawberry patch and his paradise.

Thus summer and nature are central visual concepts to Bergman. It could be argued that they are part of the pattern of crisis situations in his films. "Happiness" or "freedom" — or whatever we want to call it — is fleeting; it is only a respite, a moment's grace, always threatened and doomed to disappear. But, says Donner:

> Foreign critics have interpreted this in a more than necessarily complicated manner. They have sought the symbolic meaning of the summer theme and forgotten its actual one. They have not known what summer in Scandinavia implies. . . . [It is] mirrored in the lives of the people, in the dream of freedom, which is almost always a summer dream.

And he adds: ". . . the artist who chooses this subject is not original, finds no new symbols" (73).

Certainly it is true that the Bergman summer, to a degree, coincides with the summer of Swedish reality; certainly as such it is a cliché: short, intense, and always threatened by autumn.

But what is interesting, after all, is the charged meaning of this "Swedishness" in the film's fictive universe. This can, of course, apply to all art, but especially to that of such a pronounced auteur as Bergman, whose work constitutes a universe in which the parts are more closely related to its own fictive wholeness than to anything outside of it. Or, as Dusan Makavejev has put it: "Bergman's work is actually inimitable; for in spite of the fact that he repeatedly uses the same visual clichés, these Bergmanian clichés cannot be found in other films."[8]

Capturing the Invisible

The fact that the summer in Bergman's films is charged in accordance with a specifically Bergmanian mythology is shown by the way Bergman uses the summer light, that light which Marianne Höök refers to when she speaks of Bergman's pronounced feeling for "coloristic effects in black and white." She mentions *Smiles of a Summer Night* as an example: It "has in its extreme whiteness all the nuances of a color film and a joy in storytelling which is seldom found in movies but often in painting" (75).

We rarely notice how Bergman turns inside out those positive meanings which, in both reality and fiction, usually are associated with this "extreme whiteness."

Take, for example, the famous nightmare sequence at the beginning of *Wild Strawberries*, with its overexposed images and strong contrasts of light and shade. This overexposure admittedly leads the mind to a now rather threadbare expressionistic tradition with origins in the German cinema of the twenties. But in contrast to this tradition, which involved films made completely in the studio, Bergman's nightmare sequences are obviously filmed outdoors. The sharp contrasts between light and shade suggest a scorching, brightly lit street in the midday sun. The light — that positive summer light — has been transformed into its opposite.

Another example from the same film is the scene in which the professor witnesses a rendezvous between his wife and a man. The scene takes place in a big, dark forest, but, characteristically, in a brightly sunlit glade. The whole situation becomes an ironic idyll: summer as a dream has been transformed into summer as a nightmare.

Something similar also happens in *The Virgin Spring* (1959), in which a young maiden is raped on a naked sunlit hill. There are no dark, ominous clouds, but only a blinding, devastating light, which stands in sharp contrast to the journey on horseback depicted earlier, in which the light was soft and gentle, like the young birch trees and flowery meadows alongside the young maiden's path.

Through a Glass Darkly (1960) and *Winter Light* (1961/62) take place in extremely isolated environments — a barren island and a desolate country church — which become concrete images of an inner landscape: of the lack of communication, of the silence between God and man, between man and man. (This spiritualization of nature is also characteristic of Swedish poetry and landscape painting.) This visual asceticism, this lack of nature and milieu, is, to use Birgitta Steene's words, part of Bergman's "Gothic quality."[9]

An example of the lack of "normal" depiction of environment is the way in which Bergman chooses to begin many of his films. Thus *Fanny and Alexander* (1982) begins with a series of images of different objects — a statue, a window, a tree — accompanied by the clear, ringing sound of a clock.

These are far from being ordinary establishing shots. Rather, they are charged with a totally opposite meaning: They form an entrance or door to a completely different world.

As so often with Bergman, they are about events not visible to the eye, but, quite paradoxically, they must be shaped and experienced through the eye. It is a matter of capturing the invisible with the most visible of media.

Literary Tradition

Apart from the silent-movie tradition, Bergman is very close to Swedish literature and theater. In Donner's words: "No director has ever come to films with such a great reliance on literature" (153).

In *The Seventh Seal,* Bergman has chosen to shape his depiction of modern religious problems according to the schematic pattern of medieval morality. Here are purely allegorical features, such as the chess game with Death, and the characters — the Knight, Death, Mia, and Jof — have all the features of Christian moral archetypes.

Even when the plot takes place in the present, Bergman's films — especially the earlier ones — tend to have a touch of allegorical polish. In his 1944 film *Torment,* written by Bergman and directed by Alf Sjöberg, the Devil is found in the shape of the sadistic Latin teacher, the knight is a student, and the young maiden is the student's girlfriend.

The result is a peculiar mixture of the abstract and the concrete, the metaphysical and the realistic. This oscillation is perhaps part of Bergman's stylistic uniqueness, which he has gradually refined. One example is *Fanny and Alexander,* in which the most fantastic events are told in a seemingly straightforward, simple, and "realistic" way.

Here are found all kinds of Ovidian metamorphoses and mysteriously Swedenborgian correspondences across time and space; people and places meet and merge as in a dream and change shape. This is done, however, without the camera commenting and without making use of overexposure or other clichéd transitions to indicate the difference between dream and reality: Style and content have become one.

This is one of the film's themes: that dreams and the inexplicable and magical are in the midst of us, in the midst of everyday life and reality. Or, as Aron, son of Isak the Jew, says: "We are surrounded by realities, one outside of the other."

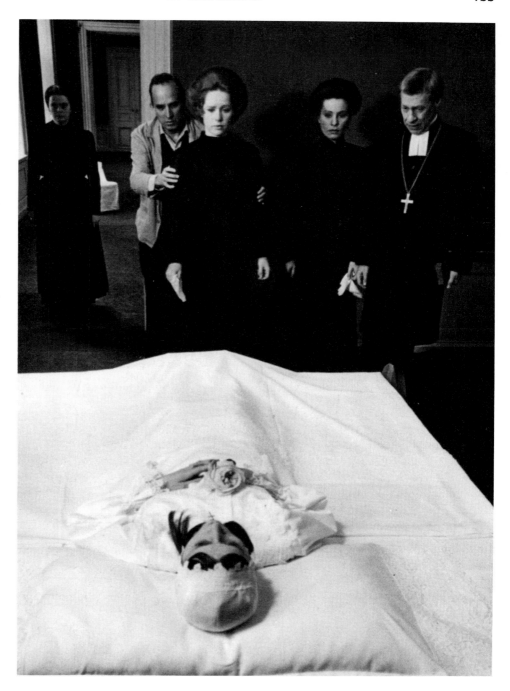

Bergman blocking Liv Ullmann in Cries and Whispers *(1971)*

But just as in Bergman's visual style, the cracks are invisible.

Bergman shares this mixture of realism and visual delusion with some of the most prominent figures of Swedish literary realism, including Carl Jonas Love Almqvist (1793–1866), August Strindberg (1849–1912), and Hjalmar Bergman (1883–1931), who all possessed a feeling for the sensual and the grotesque, the realistic and the dreamlike.[10]

Bergman's films exhibit other similarities with these authors. Especially in his earlier films, there are confrontations — reminiscent of Hjalmar Bergman — between a corrupt and cynical parental generation and an unspoiled and optimistic youth. Ingmar Bergman's movies in general have much of the earlier Bergman's pessimistic view of man as a puppet, manipulated and controlled by outside forces. Even in a cheerful film like *Smiles of a Summer Night* the characters, as Donner points out, move like marionettes in the game of love (128). And is there not also in this film a touch of Hjalmar Söderberg, the Swedish turn-of-the-century novelist who wrote that the only sure things in life are carnal pleasures and the incurable solitude of the soul?

According to Bergman himself, the closest parallels between his films and his literary antecedents are with the works of August Strindberg. There is the same unromantic nakedness in their descriptions of relations between the sexes, and perhaps some of Strindberg's views on women can be found in the films as well.

To be sure, Bergman's women, like the nature depicted in his films, are not merely "themselves" and should therefore not be judged in psychological-realistic terms. In *The Silence,* for example, the two female main characters are components in a uniquely Bergmanian mythology and as such represent opposing concepts: intellect vs. feeling, soul vs. body, "masculine" vs. "feminine." But as feminist-inspired critics have pointed out, it is striking how often even these female concepts are either vigorous sexual beings or — if they are of the more "intellectual" type — neurotic and frigid.[11]

Bergman's films also contain direct, creative borrowings from Strindberg's plays. The most obvious one is perhaps Isak Borg's dream in *Wild Strawberries.* He finds himself back in school and is declared incompetent by the examiner, who also accuses him of "some minor offenses": "insensitivity, selfishness, and ruthlessness." This is obviously inspired by *A Dream Play.* In the Strindberg drama, the Officer, who, like Isak Borg, is being awarded an honorary doctorate, is tested on his multiplication tables and fails. (We cannot help being reminded of the lawyer in *A Dream Play,* who is asked by the daughter of the god Indra what the worst thing about life on earth is. He replies: "Repetition. Doing things again. Going back." This is exactly what Isak Borg has to do — go back, remember, and look inside himself.)

Even the structure of *Wild Strawberries* is similar to that of *A Dream Play,* because Bergman, like Strindberg, uses the free associations and floating boundaries of the dream technique. In *Fanny and Alexander,* Bergman has the grandmother read aloud from the Author's Note to *A Dream Play*: "Anything can happen, everything is possible and plausible. Time and space do not exist. Against an insignificant background, the imagination spins and weaves new designs." These words become an aesthetic credo, not only for *Fanny and Alexander,* but for all Bergman's cinematic works: the film as dream play, the dream as film play.

Typically European

Strindberg, however, lies outside the boundaries of Swedish culture. And, like Strindberg, Bergman very much belongs to a European literary tradition; just think of the artistic conflict in, for example, *The Naked Night* (*Sawdust and Tinsel*), *The Magician* (1958), and *Persona* (1965), which also pervades twentieth-century literature. The metaphysical problems in Bergman's films, which though couched in Lutheran terms do not express anything specifically Swedish, by their very nature are universal. To exaggerate a bit, they express not so much belief, as doubt, perhaps an eternally human and existential *state of crisis,* a revolt against an absolute authority who might be God, fellow human beings, or marriage. "Hell is other people. . . ."

In this context, do not forget that Bergman's films, especially those of the forties, are obviously colored by the literary and philosophical movement then current in Europe (which in Sweden found expression in the "faithlessness" of the time). In the center stood, not social, but abstract beings — Sisyphos, K, suffering Humanity.[12] The Bergmanian conceptualization of people and situations displays similarities not only with a specifically Swedish cultural heritage but also with a specifically European tradition.

And perhaps, as Marianne Höök points out, this lack of anchorage in a Here and Now at least partly explains Bergman's international success (55). Thus, it is interesting that the film which brought about Bergman's international breakthrough by winning a prize at the Cannes Festival in 1956 was *Smiles of a Summer Night,* though this seemingly very "Swedish" film is actually one of Bergman's most "foreign" ones. It is inspired by eighteenth-century French comedy and is also reminiscent of Jean Renoir's film *Rules of the Game* (1939). And Bergman himself has mentioned the French director's father as a source of inspiration: "I hope that, in its best moments, it will evoke images of Renoir's and Degas' paintings."[13]

There are thus good reasons to assume that when the film received the Cannes prize, the French were at least as delighted with its familiar attributes as with all the new — exotic Swedish — attributes they didn't recognize. It might be said that Bergman, as yet another Swede in the footsteps of Strindberg, was declared "French." That would fit in with what Horace Walpole once said: "If something foreign arrives in Paris, they say that it has always been there. . . ."[14]

It is very difficult to pinpoint anything unequivocally "Swedish" in Bergman's works. Yet it is not surprising that his films, which almost singlehandedly created the reputation of Swedish cinema abroad, are also characterized as "typically Swedish," through some kind of logical non sequitur or guilt by association. It is significant that this sort of characterization has not been made in Sweden, but abroad, where most of the literature about Bergman is published.

The question is whether the Swedes themselves haven't accepted the foreign conception of Bergman as "typically Swedish" and done so uncritically, out of pure gratitude for the fact that the world has turned its face toward their nation's culture, thereby completely swallowing the legend.

The question is not so much how "Swedish" Bergman's movies are, but to what degree they have colored our perception of what is Swedish. To put it bluntly, it is not so much whether Bergman is "Swedish," but whether the Swedes, in the eyes of themselves and others, are or have become "Bergmanian."

In that case, Bergman's art has not imitated Swedish reality, as is often claimed, but, instead, reality has imitated art.

Translated by Victor Kayfetz

Notes

[1] Vernon Young, *Cinema Borealis: Ingmar Bergman and the Swedish Ethos,* New York, 1971, 216.

[2] Jörn Donner, *The Films of Ingmar Bergman,* New York, 1972.

[3] "Cries and Whispers in Socialism's Showcase," *Time,* June 7, 1976.

[4] Leif Furhammar, *Film in Sweden,* Stockholm, 1966, 22.

[5] Other U.S. distribution titles for this film were *The Treasure of Arne* and *The Three Who Were Doomed.*

[6] Marianne Höök, *Ingmar Bergman,* Stockholm, 1962, 75.

[7] As quoted in Fritiof Billquist, *Ingmar Bergman, Teatermannen och filmskaparen,* Stockholm, 1960, 196.

8 Dusan Makavejev, "An Investigation — Bergman's Non-Verbal Sequences: Sources of a Dream Film Experiment" in *Film and Dreams: An Approach to Bergman,* Vlada Petric, ed., South Salem, NY, 1981, 192.

9 Birgitta Steene, *Ingmar Bergman,* New York, 1968, 97.

10 As Steene has also pointed out; see 134.

11 See, for example, Joan Mellen, *Women and Their Sexuality in the New Film,* New York, 1973, 97–117.

12 See Donner, 13.

13 Billquist, 169.

14 Young, 146.

"MANHATTAN SURROUNDED BY INGMAR BERGMAN": THE AMERICAN RECEPTION OF A SWEDISH FILMMAKER

BIRGITTA STEENE

A native of Sweden, Birgitta Steene is Professor of Scandinavian Literature and Cinema Studies at the University of Washington and Research Professor at the University of Stockholm. She has written several books and numerous articles on Ingmar Bergman and Scandinavian cinema. She is currently engaged in an international project on Bergman and his public.

It is now almost thirty-five years ago that an American film reviewer made the following observation:

> Ingmar Bergman, as almost everybody knows by now, is the hottest director on the international scene today. . . . In New York, for example, his conquest is as complete as it is sudden. It was only last winter . . . that Manhattan began to look like an Island entirely surrounded by Ingmar Bergman. [Arlene Croce, *Commonweal,* March 11, 1960]

The American success of Bergman's films was not limited to Manhattan, of course, but spread like wildfire across the entire United States. Within a concentrated period of a few years, the American public could see such central Bergman films as *The Seventh Seal, Wild Strawberries, The Magician,* and *The Virgin Spring;* and in their wake many of his earlier works appeared, either for the first time or as second showings. Ingmar Bergman was on his way to becoming somewhat of an American cult(ural) phenomenon. Soon his films were common topics of conversation on college campuses, in film clubs and coffee shops throughout the country. Retrospective showings were in fact legion by the mid-sixties. Bergman's American distributor at the time, Janus Films Inc., reported that his films constituted more than twenty-five percent of the company's rental business and noted that a work like *The Seventh Seal* was shown on an average twice a day in the United States. The American press and publication world also responded to this interest in Bergman's films. In 1959 the *New York Times Magazine* presented him in two articles, and in the following spring, barely two years after his American breakthrough with *The Seventh Seal,* Bergman appeared on the cover of *Time.* In the same year four of his screenplays — *Smiles of a Summer Night, The Seventh Seal, Wild Strawberries,* and *The Magician* — were published together and were a Book-of-the-Month Club choice. It is remarkable that Bergman's screenplays were published first in the United States, long before any Swedish publisher brought them out in book format. This is in turn symptomatic

137

Max von Sydow (lower center) and cast members of
Ibsen's The Wild Duck *at the Royal Dramatic Theater*
of Sweden in 1972

of the fact that Ingmar Bergman's greatest public success has not been in his native country. In a 1990s Swedish study focusing on a statistically selected but very small segment of the Stockholm audience who followed a year-long retrospective of Bergman's films, it became clear that this group of Swedes considered themselves a minority in terms of their Bergman interest and often defined their position as a reaction to the negative views embraced by family members, friends, and workmates. It is fair to say that without the international, and especially the American, response to his films, Bergman would have had a hard time

achieving the status of independent filmmaker that he came to enjoy by the mid-sixties.

Yet when asked in a radio interview in March 1961 if he would not have to redefine his filmmaking approach, now that America had discovered him, Bergman gets very excited and retorts:

Wait, wait my friend. . . . It's like this. I think it's a lot of fun, all that business with foreign [attention] but I always figure and plan my films in this way, that they have to stick to the Scandinavian market, if possible. I try to represent my topics so that they address themselves to a native public or, at any rate, they shall not have to be based, financially, on any foreign revenues.

Sensitivity about his artistic integrity, which is at the root of Bergman's response, is also expressed in his early essays, such as "What Is Filmmaking" ("Detta att göra film," 1954) and "Every Film Is My Last" ("Varje film är min sista," 1959). When Bergman appeared upon the scene in the 1940s, film production in Sweden was a nonsubsidized, moneymaking, and competitive industry, on a smaller scale not unlike the structure of Hollywood. Bergman had no illusions about this: "Our films are assigned to businessmen, who at times regard them with suspicion." At the other end of the receiving spectrum was the public, who demanded to be entertained. Bergman at one time likened himself to an acrobat doing somersaults to amuse a whole string of "investors" with a stake in his art: the producers, the movie-house owners, the ticket buyers, the critics. Partly to boost his own morale, partly to clarify his artistic position, he wrote down his credo, claiming "For me there is only one loyalty — that is my loyalty to the film I am working on." However, another loyalty runs like a red thread through Bergman's many statements about his filmmaking (and theater work) over the years: his sense of loyalty to his public. Without the public, both feared and loved, the artist's greatest need would be aborted: his need to communicate. In a recent interview Bergman pinpoints this unending dialogue between himself and his viewers:

> I love the public. I always think: "I am very explicit and clear, they must understand what I mean, it's not difficult." But often I have realized that I haven't been explicit enough and simple enough. But my entire life I have worked with and for the public (S. Björkman, *Tre dar med Bergman,* 1993).

Embedded in a statement like this is perhaps one of the fundamental keys to Bergman's success with audiences all over the world. He is involved in a constant dialogue with his prospective viewers, yet he seldom woos them for opportunistic reasons. Twice he has been tempted to bring American money and American actors into his pictures, in *The Touch* and *The Serpent's Egg,* and both times the setup backfired. The gist of the matter seems to be that by remaining faithful to his Swedish context and an imaginary Swedish public, defined early in his career, Ingmar Bergman, while becoming an artist of world renown, remained faithful to himself.

Bergman and Bergman

Few audiences have paid Ingmar Bergman as much homage and respect as his American public. But when his name first appeared in the United States in the late 1940s, Americans got it confused with that of Swedish-born film star Ingrid Bergman. The two earliest presentations of the Swedish filmmaker carried headlines in the *New York Times* that alluded to this: "The Other Bergman" and "Another Bergman Gains Renown." But this was quickly to change, as can be gauged by checking a reference work like *Readers' Guide to Periodical Literature* during the second half of the 1950s. Between 1955 and 1957, Ingrid Bergman is mentioned in twelve entries, and in the next two years she appears in nine listings. During this same period there are no references at all to Ingmar Bergman. But from 1959 to 1961 the situation is different. Now the Swedish filmmaker is listed in fourteen items, both articles and interviews, while his namesake has slipped to six entries. It would, in fact, not be until 1978 that the two artists could make similar claims to American press visibility. But by then they appeared not as contending names but in a partnership undertaking. For it was in that year that Ingmar Bergman completed his film *Autumn Sonata,* with Ingrid Bergman in the leading role, thus making good a verbal agreement that the two had made more than a decade earlier.

Bibi Andersson and Lille Terselius in Shakespeare's Twelfth Night *at the Royal Dramatic Theater of Sweden in 1975*

Reception of the Early Films

It is sometimes forgotten that when Ingmar Bergman's films took New York and the country by storm in the late fifties, the Swedish filmmaker was no longer a young man and no newcomer to the film world. When *The Seventh Seal* premiered in the United States, Bergman was forty years old and had been engaged in filmmaking for almost fifteen years. He had behind him the production of more than twenty-five feature films, four scripts for films he did not direct, and a series of soap commercials made in 1951, when Swedish film studios were shut down because of a tax dispute and lockout. (This is totally unrelated to Bergman's personal controversy with Swedish tax authorities, which led to his voluntary exile in April 1976.) Although his earliest films were seldom distributed in the United States and were mostly ignored by the American press, it is possible to gather enough information about their reception to suggest some built-in American notions about Swedish thinking and Swedish filmmaking which colored Bergman's earliest reception in the United States. Some of these ideas were to be of lasting importance in terms of Bergman's image in America, for instance the view that his films expressed a national mood, a typically Swedish gloom. Other aspects seem of a more transitory nature, such as the charge that his films were speculative sexploiters.

In the Beginning Was *Torment*

Americans first encountered Bergman as a scriptwriter. The Sjöberg-Bergman film *Torment* from 1944 became in fact a cult film in New York and Los Angeles right after World War II. But in keeping with the star focus of the time, most of the attention was given to the actors. One of them — Alf Kjellin — was soon wooed by Hollywood, where he eventually became a producer of television series. His costar Mai Zetterling was snatched up by the British Rank Corporation; in the sixties she established herself as a feminist filmmaker. Before the arrival of the European postwar cinema in the fifties, it was rare that a director's name was considered a selling point in the launching of a film. Had Kjellin and Zetterling appeared in the earliest films directed by Ingmar Bergman, these works might well have attracted more attention, but Bergman was not to assemble his famous "stable of actors" until well into the 1950s (an exception is Gunnar Björnstrand). Like all Swedish film directors at the time, Bergman was dependent upon the studio system, that is, upon the availability of photographers and actors. The yearly filmmaking period was short in Sweden. With its long tradition of outdoor shooting and its seasonal employment of film actors, who were mostly recruited from the theater, films were for the most part made during a few hectic summer months. The producers were far more powerful in allocating the resources of the company than what is suggested in later accounts of Bergman's career as an auteur.

And Then There Was *Crisis*

Two weeks after the Swedish premiere of Ingmar Bergman's first directed film, *Kris* (*Crisis*, 1945), *Variety* ran a notice datelined Stockholm. Headlined "Young Girl's Troubles," the brief report refers to *Kris* as one of the highlights of that year's Swedish film production. This hardly corresponds to the real facts about its reception in the home market. Though some reviewers sensed a new directorial talent, several leading Swedish film critics dismissed the film as "a crisis" and pointed to one aspect of Bergman's artistic temperament that has always been a sore point with his Swedish public, namely, his tendency to depict emotional encounters that exceed what his own culture conceives of as normal. As one critic put it:

> There is something unbridled, nervously out of control in Bergman's imagination that makes a disquieting impression. He is thrown from one exaggeration to another and seems to be incapable of keeping a mental level of normalcy. What the Swedish cin-

ema needs in the first place are not experimenters but intelligent, rational people who can give us living human beings and essential conflicts (*Bonniers Litterära Magasin*, March 1946).

Despite such reservations about Bergman's filmmaking on the home front, *Variety*'s correspondent maintained that "while few Swedish films mean much in the world market, *Kris* looks to have a chance for usual modest returns obtained by strongest products from Sweden in the American market."

Bergman's Early Films and the Sexploiter Genre

An obvious promotional attempt to attract an American public with titillating posters and suggestive titles was made for a number of early Bergman films. *Fängelse* (Prison, 1948/49) was renamed *The Devil's Wanton* and *Kvinnors väntan* (Waiting Women, 1952) was distributed as *Secrets of Women*. The most flagrant exploitation struck two other Bergman films from the early fifties: *Sommarlek* (Summer Play, 1950; American opening, 1954) and *Sommaren med Monika* (Summer with Monika, 1953; American opening 1956). *Sommarlek*'s U.S. title, *Illicit Interlude*, tries to imply a promiscuous meeting of short duration. One might compare this with David Lean's *Brief Encounter*, which also depicts an adulterous affair but whose title carries none of the insinuated moral transgression of *Illicit Interlude*. Yet, the U.S. title change of Bergman's *Sommarlek*, which was later rectified to *Summer Interlude*, is minor compared to the liberties that the overseas distributor, Gaston Hakim Productions, took with the film in arranging additional bathing scenes to be shot on Long Island Sound. Using backlighting to emulate the silhouetted images of nude bathing associated with Swedish filmmaking, these scenes aimed at prolonging and making more explicit the erotic encounter between Bergman's young couple, the ballerina Marie and her student lover.

Bergman's Films as an American Counterimage

When the reviewer in *Newsweek* wrote apropos of *The Naked Night* that the Swedes, because of their heavy temperament, seemed incapable of producing "happy films," this was more than a critical judgment of the gloom-and-doom Bergman Swedes. It was a form of cultural displacement, the stereotyping of a counterimage to the officially happy and optimistic American society painted with words and palette by the two Normans in American culture at the time: preacher Norman Vincent Peale and artist Norman Rockwell, and endorsed by Hollywood and the American entertainment world. Bergman's early films, most of them set in contemporary times and dealing with youthful rebellion or uneasiness with bourgeois autocracy, may have triggered a negative response in America because in their explicitness they lay bare similar repressed anxieties in a nation that was trying to uphold traditional values in a postwar world.

In retrospect, the decade that witnessed Bergman's American breakthrough appears as a contradictory time in the United States, characterized by a search for both social and ontological security but replete with signs of questioning and frustration. As film critic Molly Haskell has summed up, the optimism of the fifties was "a front, the topsoil that protected the seed of rebellion that was germinating below" (*From Reverence to Rape*, 1972). When the forced optimism of the Eisenhower era collapsed in the social unrest of the following decade, the youth of the fifties were referred to as "the silent generation," in contrast to the demonstrating young people who participated in the civil rights movement and the Vietnam War demonstrations. But one might wonder if the epithet "the inward generation" would not be more appropriate, for the fifties bred, in many ways, an isolationist crowd, somewhat self-absorbed and focused on "the little world." Yet underneath their aspirations to lead the good life in middle-class suburbia lay a certain reflective questioning of the American happiness syndrome. Even Hollywood came close to exposing life behind the optimistic façade, thus exemplifying what Michel Foucault has referred to as cracks in the social fabric, through which deviations from the dominant culture can seep in. It is not unusual in American film melodrama of the fifties to have the nostalgic or regressive forces, characterizing society at large, meet resistance in the private sphere. The many male antiheroes that appear in American films of the fifties may constitute such a subversion of official norms. The lead character no longer embodies a traditional American ideal — the masculine action hero who takes charge of a problem situation. Instead we find the hesitant sheriff (Gary Cooper) and silent Robert Prewitt (Montgomery Clift) in Fred Zinnemann's *High Noon* and *From Here to Eternity;* the passive Kirby (Rock Hudson) in Douglas Sirk's *All That Heaven Allows;* the morose and rebellious teenager Jim (James Dean) in Nicholas Ray's *Rebel without a Cause.* All of these males break with the image of the masculine, paternal, and secure male that the times and President Eisenhower's persona prescribed. The men in these films are either insecure, frustrated, and oversensitive or, like Jim's father in *Rebel,* henpecked. Nor do the women fulfill their expected roles, a fact that has made Brandon French (*On the Verge of Revolt,* 1978) see these films as symptomatic of "a tumultuous dissatisfaction on the part of both men and women with a society which indiscriminately channels their passionate energy into middle-class marriages — marriages which shackle couples to an economic grindstone that annihilates individual identity and love."

Hollywood, believing its mission to be to entertain the masses and to uphold public morality, worked to seal the cracks. Basically realistic melodramas like *Rebel without a Cause* were given forced happy endings. But such closures create uneasiness in the spectator. As Robert Ray has noted in his book *A Certain Tendency of the Hollywood Cinema, 1930–1980*: "The more realistically the problem pictures portrayed postwar

A scene from Hamlet *at the Royal Dramatic Theater of Sweden in 1986, presented at the Brooklyn Academy of Music in 1988*

America's sociological crises, the more they enabled the audience to recognize the transparently mythological status of their reconciliations." That the public grew increasingly skeptical of Hollywood's optimistic cop-outs might help explain why a dark problem film like Bergman's *Det sjunde inseglet* (*The Seventh Seal*) could elicit such a strong positive response from relatively large segments of the American public. Its ending, juxtaposing the Dance of Death motif and the survival of the family of Jof, Mia, and Mikael, was no superimposed closure, but grew out of the dramatic and visual dichotomies of the story, where religious questing, love, and survival are countered by superstition, plague, and death, with the white and the black pieces on the chessboard serving as a repeated imagistic emblem.

Bergman's American Breakthrough

It has been said about Swedish art and outlook that they are not much given to understatement, suggestion, or indirection but are expressed with an unabashed openness that to a non-Swede can appear both naïve and shocking or serve as a pointed exposure of sensitive or taboo areas. Bergman's films of the early fifties centered on issues that for most Americans at that time could not be handled so explicitly and broke with the codes established for mainstream cinema. At the same time these early films often exposed an artistic ambition still in the making. Their uneven quality made it much easier to dismiss them and downgrade them to the fare of the local soft-porno theater. But since Bergman's primary concern was not — unlike, for instance, Vilgot Sjöman in *I Am Curious (Yellow)* — to challenge the voyeuristic sex barrier of the film medium, these early films did not do very well as porno pictures either. It is in fact hard to imagine a less auspicious entrance on the American market than Ingmar Bergman's first encounter with U.S. culture. Yet by the end of the 1950s his name as a filmmaker was respected and well known throughout the United States.

There is an ironic paradox in the fact that when Bergman worked in the realistic mode in his early films, set in the contemporary world, these films were often received by American reviewers in a caustic or facetious way, but when he fulfilled his longtime ambition to make a metaphysical film like *The Seventh Seal,* he displeased his own countrymen, whereas the American public accepted him as a *directeur du conscience* who raised pertinent and ageless issues. What then were some of the reasons for the positive American response to *The Seventh Seal,* the film that, more than any, was a turning point in Bergman's reception in the United States?

The Packaging and Reception of *The Seventh Seal*

In 1956, Bergman's turn-of-the-century costume comedy *Smiles of a Summer Night* received the coveted jury prize in Cannes. Soon afterward he began shooting *The Seventh Seal,* which opened in Sweden in February 1957. Although it received rather mixed reviews in the Swedish press, the film was hailed by French cinéastes in Paris as "a cinematic Faust" (Eric Rohmer, *Arts,* April 1957). *The Seventh Seal* was on its way to the international circuit. But by the time it arrived in New York, in October 1958, Bergman had already released his next two films in Sweden: *Smultronstället* (*Wild Strawberries,* 1957; U.S.

opening, 1959) and *Nära livet* (*Brink of Life,* 1957; U.S. opening, 1959), and was awaiting the premiere of *Ansiktet* (*The Magician,* 1958; U.S. opening, 1959). One reason for Bergman's impact on American audiences in the late fifties was the concentrated packaging with which his films from the second half of the decade were marketed in the U.S. It meant, for one thing, that his crew of actors, which had by now begun to form a Bergman ensemble — Max von Sydow, Bibi Andersson, Ingrid Thulin, Gunnar Björnstrand — in a short time became well-known faces to American audiences. This was not unimportant in the star-studded United States. Furthermore, in this group of films Bergman expressed an artistic identity that fascinated through its subjective power. Here, too, Bergman could be said to fit into an American cultural pattern, for despite its mass-media orientation American culture is basically individualistic in its evaluations of art.

That the abstract morality-play structure of Bergman's *The Seventh Seal* made the film transcend national and social boundaries was clearly enunciated in most major American reviews. The rarity of making a metaphysical quest the center of a film, using a fictional rather than a historical character as the protagonist, was often noted by referring to the Knight, the main character in the film, as an Everyman figure. Bosley Crowther's discussion of *The Seventh Seal* in his book *The Great Films: Fifty Golden Years of Motion Pictures* (1967) may serve as an example:

The Seventh Seal is essentially the story of a lonely man's search for God — or perhaps it might better be said, the story of a man's search for meaning in life. Its hero is seeking the Answer. "I want knowledge, not belief," he cries, "not [blind] faith, not suppositions, but knowledge!" This ageless cry of anguish is the theme of only a few great films. And the extraordinary thing about this one is the forcefulness with which it conveys the magnitude of its abstract ideas with visual images, the manner in which it makes you fathom the loneliness of man, the mystery of God, the fearless shadow that lies between life and death, the hideousness of superstition, and the piteousness of blind faith.

According to Michael Roemer, film critic, in *The Reporter*, February 15, 1962, Bergman could — by making the Knight (Antonius Block) a non-historical figure — make the audience sense the timelessness of the theme of *The Seventh Seal*. Antonius Block was not a reconstructed person from the past but a subjectively conceived character whose inner life was more important than some of the physical events around him:

> The rendering of reality [in the film] is subjective. Antonius Block is no medieval knight but a modern man trying to find his way past doubt and despair. . . . While the setting and some of the details are treated realistically, no attempt is made to give the story an objective reality.

Though several Swedish critics had expressed similar views, emphasizing in particular Bergman's use of a black-and-white, almost ascetic visual style and noting its organic affinity to the film's serious topic, some remained skeptical and ambivalent about *The Seventh Seal*. One critic (Hanserik Hjertén) felt that Bergman "had made a horror film for children instead of a mature exposé and that he himself has functioned like a frightened child." The film became the object of a lively debate in Swedish mass media but has never attained the near-cult status it received in the United States, where, to quote one American critic, "it had a tremendous impact on a whole generation of young intellectuals" (Croce).

The Seventh Seal and Elitist versus Popular Aesthetics

In retrospect, one can surmise from the reception of *The Seventh Seal* in the United States and in Sweden that Bergman's film encountered two au-diences, whose culture differed in some central ways. In the Swedish (and European) tradition of dividing artistic expression and its consumers into two camps, high or polite culture and low or popular culture, and using bourgeois values as a measure, Matthew Arnold's elitist definition was still normative in the 1950s. In Arnold's nomenclature, "culture" *excluded* all forms of popular entertainment and, representing the highest forms of art, it was something that trickled down to the masses. In such a definition of "culture," the past dictated the taste of the present. Between Swedish viewers and Bergman's *The Seventh Seal* stood a great many works in the same metaphysical genre, in film and in literature: Sjöström's *The Phantom Carriage* (1921), Strindberg's *The Saga of the Folkungs* (1901), Rune Lindström's *The Road to Heaven* (1942), Stig Dagerman's *The Man Condemned to Death* (1948), and Pär Lagerkvist's *Barabbas* (1951). These earlier works detracted from the novelty of *The Seventh Seal* in that they included matters that were very similar, either to the setting and composition of Bergman's film or to its major theme — the Knight's quest and its existential and eschatological ramifications. But none of them oscillated as drastically (if at all) between high tragedy and low comedy as *The Seventh Seal*. This made it difficult for the Swedish critics to admit the film into the realm of Arnoldian culture — its humor was much too close to the popular farce or burlesque referred to as *buskteater*. While always concerned about not prostituting his art, Bergman was also aware, from the start, of working in a mass medium: "I do not create my work for my own or a few people's moral education but for the entertainment of millions." Swedish critics of *The Seventh Seal* recognized but did not always condone Bergman's conscious attempt to perform a "Shakespearean" feat of balancing between high culture and the world of popular art.

In Arnoldian aesthetics a recipient of an artistic product sees the function of art as an objectification process and the function of criticism as an activity reinforcing an artistic canon. The policy thrust of the Swedish cinema since its early inception had been to "raise" the new art above the medium's popular origins. Hence its first movie mogul, Charles Magnusson, decided to invite directors trained in the theater (a more prestigious art) to join his film company, Svenska Bio, and urged them to look to classical works in Swedish literature as a basis for good scripts.

In the beginning of his film career Bergman liked to challenge elitist aestheticism and spoke with delight about the cinema's roots in popular forms of entertainment, such as the circus, vaudeville, and the broadsheet:

> There is nothing shameful or degrading about the cinema having been at one time a peep show entertainment, a clownish and conjuring art. But it is wrong and denigrating to wish to deny its origin and make it lose its sense of magic and its playful qualities that are so stimulating to our imagination (*Biografbladet* 3, 1947).

In a film like *The Naked Night,* which has the subtitle *A Broadsheet for Film,* Bergman exposes the rivalry between highbrow culture and popular entertainment by letting the representatives of the theater meet the members of the circus. Bergman's sympathies are clearly on the side of the circus people and popular culture.

Yet at the same time Bergman has always — his own statements to the contrary — had a highbrow literary anchoring. This was simply part of his mother's milk in the educated upper-middle-class environment he grew up in. When he enrolled at Stockholm University, he chose to study literature. His theatrical activity had, from the start, a clearly classical preference, in terms of both the repertory at large and his own dramatic contributions. His great mentor was August Strindberg, hardly known for his attempts at popular entertainment, except in the novel *The People of Hemsö.* However, a look at the program notes written for some of the amateur productions for his first stage, Mäster Olofsgården in Stockholm, reveals also — as do his comments during his first two years as a professionally hired theater manager (1946–48) in Hälsingborg — that Bergman never lost sight of his potential public, defining it as an audience who demanded and had a right to be entertained in both sophisticated and popular ways. In his artistic credo "Every Film Is My Last," his first commandment is "Thou shalt always be entertaining."

Bergman was fortunate in arriving at Svensk Filmindustri at a time that was not only booming in terms of film production but also fixated on the idea of creating a new golden age for Swedish cinema. This renaissance, it was assumed, would come through the encouragement of good screenplays, solicited from literary writers. It was a harkening back to the time in the early twenties when directors Sjöström and Stiller had put Swedish filmmaking on the international map by adapting Selma Lagerlöf's novels and novellas for the screen. In such a context, Ingmar Bergman's scripts, which read like literary pieces, came as a virtual answer to the film industry's prayers. At a time when few Swedish writers wished to condescend to writing for the cinema, since it was still considered a lowbrow art form, a young rebelling son of a church pastor from socially prestigious Östermalm in Stockholm declared his confidence in the film medium, yet at the same time pointed out his strong affinity with modern classics in Swedish literature: August Strindberg, Selma Lagerlöf (subject of his gymnasium graduation paper), and Hjalmar Bergman. Bergman defined himself as a middlebrow, applying the criteria of high culture to the entertainment demand of the film medium.

One should not underestimate the importance of Bergman's middlebrow status in terms of his impact on American audiences. His films became the answer to a cultural development that was the opposite of that of Europe. American society had favored popular culture ever since the days of westward expansion, which involved large groups of immigrants who knew no or little

English and who had seldom partaken of the high culture of their countries of origin. Many of them found their artistic voice in different forms of popular culture: ethnic amateur theater, choirs, vaudeville shows, circus performances, and the new film medium. In doing so they appropriated their own past experiences and used them in the present. In fact, Baudrillard's (postmodern) discussion of the rejection of preconceived notions of art and artistic activity in favor of the exercise of art as a subjective and communal activity applies here.

The American response to *The Seventh Seal* was not weighed down by a plethora of intertextual references to earlier works in Swedish cinema and literature. Furthermore the U.S. reception indicates little difficulty with the subjective element and impact of the film. Bergman's personal voice was acknowledged but, unlike the Swedish critique, it was not labeled "Bergman's religious hangover," which is to say that it was not seen as a self-centered and outdated matter. American viewers also seem to have been more directly and openly moved by the film, and to have seen it as a cinematic expression that allowed them to appropriate their own past by participating in the making of art and myth. *The Seventh Seal* apparently touched a chord in the American consciousness of the 1950s.

Ingmar Bergman, the *auteur du cinéma*

The American public encountered Bergman's major films of the fifties over a few years. This forms a parallel to the concentrated postwar experience by cineasts in Paris of a backlog of American films of the forties, which resulted in the formulation of "la politique des auteurs." Originating among a group of would-be filmmakers and critics that assembled around the French journal *Cahiers du Cinéma,* the auteur concept was introduced to American film viewers by Andrew Sarris, reviewer for the *Village Voice,* and later editor-in-chief for a few years of an English-speaking

Peter Stormare (kneeling) and Per Myrberg in the ghost scene of Hamlet *at the Royal Dramatic Theater of Sweden in 1986, presented at the Brooklyn Academy of Music in 1988*

edition of *Cahiers*. In an interview from 1973 (*Film Heritage* 8:4) Sarris explains "la politique des auteurs" as an editorial policy:

> The whole idea was that we weren't going to review films one at a time, isolated. We were going to look at the works of groups of certain directors and see if we could find stylistic coordinates. The ones in which we did find them, they were major; and the ones we didn't, they were minor. . . . You can tell a La Cava movie, a McCarey movie, a Capra movie, a Ford movie, a Wyler movie. . . . I consider Bergman and Fellini and maybe Antonioni *auteur*.

Sarris practiced the auteur approach about as long as his enthusiasm for Bergman's film art lasted — until the mid-sixties. With the arrival of *Persona* in 1966, his Bergman interest dwindled. But his attention to the films of the late fifties was of crucial importance in changing Bergman's status in America, most particularly his long review article on *The Seventh Seal* in the newly founded journal *Film Culture* in 1958, in which he referred to the movie as the first truly existential film in the history of the cinema. Though Sarris was later to stress the auteur concept as a matter of film style rather than content, his presentation of *The Seventh Seal* focused on its philosophical theme, discussing the work as "a remarkably intricate film with many layers of meaning." The thematic aspect of Bergman's films has remained the central American focus. Moral, religious, and metaphysical problems have aroused more discussions and far more written analyses than matters of style and visual language. While this in turn has created some negative responses among American film academicians and cineasts, disclaiming Bergman as a middlebrow filmmaker and denying him importance as a stylistic pioneer, it does not detract from the fact that his films by and large have had unusually broad audience support in the United States, often stretching beyond college campuses and big-city intellectual enclaves.

Hollywood's Declining Role and Bergman's Breakthrough

Ingmar Bergman's films arrived in the United States at a time when both the production form and the image of the Hollywood film had begun to undergo change. True, Hollywood's position in American culture was still strong in the 1950s. But competition from television, the arrival of European postwar cinema on the American market, and the emergence of a number of independent producers and filmmakers were factors that soon would challenge the classical Hollywood studio system and break down its realm of moguls. The enhancement of the role of the director, brought about by the auteur perspective, did much to expose a filmmaker like Ingmar Bergman, but it also gave increasing artistic status to a long line of still-active Hollywood directors. It toned down the role played by production forces and undermined Hollywood's view of itself as the fortress of popular entertainment, with the studio system as its powerful core.

Yet the challenge of the Hollywood system helped endorse the feature film as a legitimate artistic expression among America's intellectuals. Film studies now became an acceptable subject in U.S. colleges and universities, where the clientele kept growing as the postwar generation of students was followed by the babyboomers. The universities expanded into academic megatowns, and the need for large survey courses increased steadily. Cinema studies could help fulfill this demand as hundreds of students could be gathered in large lecture halls with 16-millimeter projection facilities. Film course offerings were often administered through language and literature departments, who influenced the pedagogical methodology used in teaching the new subject. François Truffaut's statement about Ingmar Bergman as a filmmaker who used his visual talent as a novelist might use his pen served as a kind of general norm in this relatively early but decisive phase of American cinema-studies programs. "La politique des auteurs" established itself, together with the history of the cinema, as an indisputable approach to the subject. It paved the way for courses on individual filmmakers, which flourished in colleges during the sixties and seventies. In such courses, Bergman's works usually held a central position, along with the oeuvres of Hitchcock, Buñuel, Kurosawa, Fellini, Antonioni, and Godard.

As a result of the upgraded status of moviemaking, the cinema began to be viewed as a cultural barometer that could be incorporated into other cultural contexts. In this way Bergman's works were used as a basis in psychoanalytical discussions. Thus, in Erik H. Eriksson's analysis of the different ages of man (*Daedalus*, Spring 1976), Bergman's film about the aging professor of medicine, Isak Borg, in *Wild Strawberries* serves as a focal point. American theologians derived Lutheran and Kierkegaardian discourses from *The Seventh Seal* and the trilogy from the early sixties, *Såsom i en spegel* (*Through a Glass Darkly*, 1960), *Nattvardsgästerna* (*Winter Light*, 1961/62), and *Tystnaden* (*The Silence*, 1962). Theology professor Arthur Gibson's book about God's silence in Bergman's films (*The Silence of God*, 1962) established the pattern for a great many American articles and dissertations on the religious anchoring of Bergman's films that went far beyond their visual representation. During the second half of the sixties, especially after the premiere of *Vargtimmen* (*Hour of the Wolf*, 1968) Bergman's own psyche as camouflaged in his cinematic characters drew the attention of Freudian and Jungian scholars (for example, Frank Gado, *The Passion of Ingmar Bergman*, 1987). In the 1970s, after the appearance of *Viskningar och rop* (*Cries and Whispers*, 1971), his portrayal of women came under the scrutiny of a Marxist feminist, Joan Mellen (*Women and Sexuality in the New Film*, 1974). Furthermore, Bergman's own scripts attracted critics with a literary anchoring. There have been, too, a number of American studies of Bergman that have used criteria established in film aesthetics or film theory. What has made his position unique in the United States is the degree to which his works have been disseminated and used in different areas of cultural life.

After World War II one can speak not only of an Americanization of European culture, that is, a spread of popular art forms and expressions from the United States across the Atlantic, but also of a reverse process, the Europeanization of the American cinema. European postwar cinema, from neorealism to modernistic film, fueled impulses toward experimental and sophisticated new film art in the United States. Somewhere in this transition from the classical entertainment film, controlled by Hollywood, to the modernistic new American cinema, Bergman's films, at least the ones prior to *Persona,* came to constitute a middle ground. His films filled a need to both broaden and deepen the philosophical and visual radius of filmmaking and moviegoing in America while still maintaining a rapport with a large public.

Bergman's Films: American Melodrama or European Art Film?

When Ingmar Bergman was first employed at Svensk Filmindustri (SF) in the early 1940s, it was as a reader in the production company's manuscript department, referred to in trade jargon as "the cemetery of illusions." Bergman's boss was the strong-willed widow of playwright, novelist, and scriptwriter Hjalmar Bergman (no kin to Ingmar). Stina Bergman had accompanied her husband to Hollywood in the 1920s and had studied American scriptwriting. Back in Sweden she wrote an (undated) manual titled *Some Advice About Writing for the Cinema.* Though quite elementary in its approach, it focuses on the importance of good plot development and characterization, and outlines a narrative structure that follows the conventions set up in American filmmaking, aiming at drawing the audience into the world of the film by structuring a sealed-in story with a beginning, a middle, and an end. Stina Bergman encouraged her young protégé to write film scripts and offered him her summer place in the Stockholm archipelago as a retreat. The result was, among other things, the script for *Hets* (*Torment*), which was filmed as part of Svensk Filmindustri's twenty-fifth anniversary, using the best cast and film crew that could be assembled. Though the film was directed by Alf Sjöberg, its opening catapulted Ingmar Bergman's name into the media, and it was *his* story rather than Sjöberg's direction that was debated in the press. It is a story that follows the pattern of an American melodrama, or is, in the words of an American reviewer, "a suspiciously intimate tale" about a young high-school student's rebellion and love affair. The screenplay (and film) provides an instructive comparison with Nicholas Ray's *Rebel without a Cause* from 1956. Both films use traditional melodramatic features: a love story that permits the male hero (Vidgren and Jim) to enter an emotional sphere; a psychological conflict that assumes moral proportions and employs a stereotypical division of people into good and evil. Both stories follow the melodramatic pattern of an erupting crisis followed by a return to the status quo, with a forced ending as a result. Both sacrifice the victims in the plot in order to bring about an acceptable closure. Berta, Vidgren's lover, has no future in his social context and is eliminated. Plato, the younger schoolmate and idolater of Jim is a liability to his growth, a mentorship assumed too early, and is killed. Both films include tragic misfits, only to marginalize them in the end. But it was Sjöberg, and not Bergman, who added the happy resolution to *Torment*, the superintendent's visit to Berta's apartment, where Vidgren is staying. In the script the final scene takes place in the schoolyard on a rainy day, as Vidgren watches his classmates graduate. He is still an outsider in his society and Bergman does not suggest a solution to his situation. Sjöberg's conciliatory ending is more in keeping with a Hollywood pattern at the time.

Up to the making of *The Seventh Seal* in 1956–57, Bergman focused much of his attention on the young couple, sometimes predestined, as in French noir films of the late thirties, to remain outsiders in society, sometimes finding strength in their relationship to face members of established society, and always yearning for freedom of their own, a common theme in Swedish filmmaking, referred to as *utbrytningsdrömmen* (the dream of breaking away). This desire or need to be "on the road" became a dramaturgical device in Bergman's films of the late fifties, which center around a journey as both a physical undertaking and a psychological or metaphysical crisis. The anxiety of the crusader Antonius Block in *The Seventh Seal* is linked to a ten-year quest in the Holy Land; the depiction of the troubled seventy-six-year-old Isak Borg in *Wild Strawberries* takes the outer form of a journey between Stockholm and the university town of Lund; Albert Emanuel Vogler's magical displays in *The Magician* form the rationale behind his troupe's travels through nineteenth-century Sweden; and the tale of a young virgin's violent death in *The Virgin Spring* takes place during a medieval summer ride to church. To represent the physical action in a film as a journey is one of cinema's oldest conventions, capitalizing on the uniqueness of the film medium: to show movement in time and space. The classical Hollywood film built a whole genre, the Western, on travel into pioneer country, and the narrative device was to give name to a later American genre, road movies.

The journey as a quest is an old literary device as well, dating back to the *Odyssey* and the *Iliad*, and represented in Scandinavian literature by the Viking sagas. With the educational novel (Bildungsroman), journeying becomes an initiation into adulthood. Young vagabonds appear in major American literary works of the fifties: Holden Caulfield in Salinger's *Catcher in the Rye*, Nabokov's Humbert Humbert and nymphette Lolita's wild journey through motel rooms, and the protagonists in beatnik fiction, foremost of course Jack Kerouac's *On the Road*.

In such Bergman works as *The Seventh Seal* and *Wild Strawberries*, where traveling takes an inward turn and becomes an exploration of an inner territory, the initial visual contours are the

The final scene of Hamlet *at the Royal Dramatic Theater of Sweden in 1986, presented at the Brooklyn Academy of Music in 1988*

abstracted landscape of rocks in *The Seventh Seal,* suggesting an atavistic world, and the expressionistic pattern of a nightmare in *Wild Strawberries.* Though both of these "landscapes" are more symbolic than realistic, the dramaturgical use of the journey, with its anchoring in a representational world of physical and psychological verisimilitude, links Bergman's filmmaking to narrative patterns easily recognizable to American audiences.

The Assimilation of Ingmar Bergman

On a superficial level Bergman's American reputation has been noticeable for decades to just about every Swede traveling in the United States.

The first topic of conversation in meeting the American public has been Ingmar Bergman. Because of the frequency of such casual experiences one can surmise that the Swedish director has come to signify both a filmmaker and a concept in America. When Southern Methodist University, in Texas, selected Ingmar Bergman to become the first recipient of the Alger H. Meadows Award for Excellence in the Arts (1981), the jury explained their choice by stating that Bergman's artistic contributions had helped "articulate a new view on man in our time." For the American public, more than for others, Bergman's films were to constitute "a strong intellectual passion" (Crowther) and a new philosophical questioning that addressed some of the existential issues un-

Anita Björk (standing) and Stina Ekblad in Yukio Mishima's Madame de Sade *at the Royal Dramatic Theater of Sweden in 1989, presented at the Brooklyn Academy of Music in 1993*

derlying the social tensions of the time. Beneath the hippie culture and the flower power movement of the sixties lay a questioning of the moral and religious values of traditional Anglo-American life, which has great similarities with Bergman's Protestant origin. In the late fifties there is, then, a peculiar cultural paradox in terms of Ingmar Bergman's impact in the United States and in his own country. His earliest Swedish biographer, Marianne Höök, addresses in her 1962 book, *Ingmar Bergman,* what she sensed to be Bergman's anomaly as a contemporary Swedish artist, that is, the fact that he had, because of the clerical background of his family, grown up on a cultural reservation out of touch with modern Swedish society. To secularized Swedes "his thoughts and his problems are outdated. They actually belong to our grandparents' generation." But the American college crowd, where most of Bergman's devotees were to be found, saw in his film art an expression of their own questioning of established religious patterns in their society.

Philosophical affinity alone does not explain the unique position of Ingmar Bergman in America. The phenomenon has its visual element as well, first and foremost in certain pictorial references that have become emblematic, for example, the chess game between the Knight and Death in *The Seventh Seal* and the Dance of Death vignette at the end of the film; the memory of Isak Borg as he sees his parents in the tranquil summer landscape in *Wild Strawberries;* the merging of the two women's faces in *Persona;* the pietà shot of the servant holding the dying Agnes in *Cries and Whispers.* Together with the thematic focus of these films, such visual moments have laid the foundation of a particular Bergman context which has penetrated into the American cultural consciousness to such an extent that it surfaces not only as intertextual references in Woody Allen's films and as amusing pastiche in the student spoof *Da Duwe* but also as a humorous or self-ironic purpose of American postcard and syndicated comic-strip artists. That is to say, a Bergman film like *The Seventh Seal* has a cultural frame of reference that transcends the medium, the time, and the filmmaker's original intentions with the work. This is an example of how a cultural expression is assimilated by another culture as if it were a native product.

Epilogue. *Skammen* (*Shame*): An American Response

Unlike the case in the United States, Bergman's films, even when they caused debate and gained a certain notoriety, have seldom reached impressive box office figures in Sweden. An exception is *Tystnaden* (*The Silence*, 1962) which caught the interest of the Swedish Censorship Board and broke through the established sex barrier. When released uncut, the film attracted incredible attendance by Swedish standards: 1,459,031 tickets sold. Its nearest competitor that year was the annual installment of an indigenous "pilsner farce" film about the country buffoon Åsa-Nisse (about 500,000 tickets sold). But *Tystnaden*'s record is an exception for a Bergman film in Sweden. Thus four times more tickets were sold for the Åsa-Nisse film of 1967 than for Bergman's *Persona* (110,725 tickets) and three times as many in 1968, when *Vargtimmen* (*Hour of the Wolf*) premiered in Sweden (105,000 tickets).

In 1968, however, Bergman's *Skammen* (*Shame*), a film about an island community caught in a guerrilla war, opened in Stockholm. The release coincided with an escalation of the Vietnam War, and the film landed amidst strong Swedish protests against U.S. involvement in that conflict. Again, the discussion helped ticket sales, and a purported 202,632 Swedes attended during *Shame*'s first run. What such a figure cannot reveal to us is the response of the audience to the film. But the motivation for many of the spectators seems clear enough, since a high ticket sale for a Bergman film always seems to coincide with controversial media attention. One can conclude that a fair number of the Swedish spectators of *Shame* was not interested in a new Bergman film per se but were curious about a product that had been critiqued and debated in the press. In that debate Bergman had been accused of failing the

cause; his film showed guerrilla fighting without identifying the combatants in terms of an actual war situation and without taking sides. Author Sara Lidman, the active pro-FNL voice in the debate, concluded (*Aftonbladet*, October 7, 1968) that Bergman should have realized that "some liberation wars are justified." Instead he got sidetracked into making another film about neurotic artists.

The Swedish debate about *Shame* was heated but far from one-sided. It pitted the notion of the *engagé* artist, committed to social and political issues, against questions of artistic integrity. *Shame* was called "a dangerous, reactionary film" (U. Thorpe, *Aftonbladet*, October 28, 1968). Bergman himself added fuel to the debate by publishing a brief interview with himself under his old pseudonym, Ernest Riffe (*Expressen*, September 25, 1968; *Chaplin* 84:1968). Bergman/ Riffe declared himself a nonpolitical person who only belonged "to the party of scared people," and in another context, on Swedish state television (September 29, 1968) he added that artists should not take sides but "shall exist to reflect human complications, behavior, and events."

This politicized debate took a different turn in the New York reception of the film. Fundamentally, the polarization involved established critical positions. The warfare between *New Yorker* reviewer Pauline Kael, an avowed anti-auteur critic, and Andrew Sarris, an auteur critic manqué, crystallized in their respective responses to *Shame*. Kael performed a critical *volte-face* in her view of Bergman's filmmaking, seeing *Shame* as a significant departure from his earlier inner-oriented focus; in a glowing review (December 28, 1968) she admitted him to her pantheon of socially responsible, realistic filmmakers. Andrew Sarris was now in his most aggressive anti-Bergman phase and dismissed *Shame* as a poorly made war film filled with ridiculous "boom-boom theatrics." Bergman, whom Sarris a few years earlier had relabeled a competent craftsman rather than a major filmmaker (a parallel again between Sarris and the *Cahiers* group, who had dethroned Bergman after *The Virgin Spring* in opened 1960), was now further demoted to a not very good cinematic pyromaniac.

What the American public thought —*Shame* was a modest popular success in the United States upon its first release — is really unknown. But there happens to be a story of *Shame* and an American soldier. Though hardly a piece of scholarly evidence in this discussion of the U.S. reception of Bergman, it can function as a tribute to the American public for being more persistently responsive to the films of Ingmar Bergman than any other national group. The story is also an example of the cultural assimilation process: the appropriation of a foreign artistic product as part of one's own life situation.

The story unfolded on an airplane flight between San Francisco and Seattle in the summer of *1969. Shame* was playing in San Francisco at the time. I had given a Bergman lecture at Berkeley and was on my way home. Seated next to me on the plane was a young man in uniform; as it turned out he was an art history graduate student in his mid-twenties, now on his way to Fort Lewis for further transportation to the war in Vietnam. Expressing some of his fears and anxiety about the war — he had been drafted under protest —

the young soldier suddenly said: "I saw a film the other day that captured much of how I feel about this war. It was called *Shame,* a film by Ingmar Bergman. I wanted to go to a lecture about him last night, but my sister came to visit." He then made a gesture toward the back of the plane and added: "There are several guys back there who saw it with me and felt the same. To be hit on the head like that. Do you know Bergman's work?"

The ironic coincidence of sitting next to an unknown person who had missed my Bergman lecture was overshadowed completely by his response to Bergman's film. The charges of irrelevance that had been leveled against *Shame* by Bergman's *engagé* critics in Sweden faded before the personal impact that the film had had on an American soldier facing a real war. By comparison, the rhetoric of Sara Lidman seemed ridiculous and self-righteous, and the bickering of Pauline Kael and Andrew Sarris almost self-indulgent. Instead, Bergman's own words in the Swedish TV interview on *Shame* now seemed to have reached its right listener: "artists . . . shall be of some kind of help or some kind of support or moral enlightenment or self-examination."

WINTER SONGS

JOHN LAHR

John Lahr is a playwright and the theater critic for The New Yorker. *He is the author of* The Cowardly Lion, *a biography of his father, Bert Lahr, and of* Prick Up Your Ears, *a biography of Joe Orton.*

IN INGMAR BERGMAN'S MAJESTIC PRODUCTION OF SHAKEspeare's *The Winter's Tale* at the Royal Dramatic Theater in Stockholm, the play begins with the program. In it Bergman pretends to be the translator of a letter (actually, it's by Bergman himself) written in 1925 by a German professor who was returning a nineteenth-century theater poster to the Royal Library of Stockholm. The poster is reproduced on the opposite page. It announces *The Winter's Tale* as part of Miss Ulrika Sofias's nineteenth-birthday celebration, over Christmas, in the Grand Hall of Hugo Löwenstierna's hunting castle. The professor has underlined one of the cast, the writer Jonas Love Almqvist, who has a bit part, and, in passing, mentions that another professor considered him "as good as Strindberg." On that throwaway, faux-naïf sentence the full weight of Bergman's knowing, gorgeous production rests; his *Winter's Tale* is presented as part of Löwenstierna's Christmas festivities. (The production comes to the Brooklyn Academy of Music next May [1995], along with Bergman's *Madame de Sade* and, possibly, *The Misanthrope*.)

Almqvist (1793–1866) is one of Sweden's great literary figures; his poetry, novels, songs, and progressive educational ideas made him one of the most controversial figures of his day. Almqvist was an early champion of Shakespeare in Sweden, so his presence at this Christmas production has some historical rationale. Bergman uses Almqvist's music, which delicately mixes Romantic melancholy with Christian idealism, to frame in a kind of lyric embrace Shakespeare's perplexing tale of murderous jealousy and improbable redemption. Almqvist songs begin and end each of the play's two acts, and intensify the realms of regret and spiritual longing that Bergman meticulously explores. And Almqvist's own story hovers around this haunted play like yet another ghost. Almqvist, like Leontes, seems to have perpetrated an act of absurd violence: he was accused of killing a moneylender in 1851 and fled to America, where he lived until 1865. He died an outcast, protesting his innocence, in Bremen, Germany, in 1866, and his body was not returned to Sweden until 1901. The conceit of a Christmas celebration gives Bergman a brilliant scenic framework with

155

Bergman in rehearsal with Stina Ekblad (seated) and Marie Richardsson on the set of Madame de Sade *at the Royal Dramatic Theater of Sweden in 1989, presented at the Brooklyn Academy of Music in 1993*

which to keep the play's polarities of tragedy and joy, loss and rebirth always dynamically visible, and the stunning complexity of his structure perfectly suits the arabesque quality of Shakespeare's writing in the late plays.

When the audience takes its seats, the pre-play festivities are already in progress, and the Grand Hall of the hunting castle turns out to be a subtle replica of the Marble Hall of the Royal Dramatic Theater. The theater's Art Nouveau windows, its gold Egyptian light fittings, its gilt columns, and even part of Carl Larsson's ceiling fresco, "The Birth of Drama," are reproduced in Lennart Mörk's elegant set. The world of the play and the world of the theater are one. In a swirl of song, dance, and party hubbub the guests foreshadow aspects of their Shakespearean personae. The shambolic man struggling with his lines will become Autolycus (Reine Brynolfsson). The no-nonsense lady calling for the songs to begin and leading a young boy across the stage will be the tenacious Paulina (Bibi Andersson), who faces up to Leontes. A youngster, who will play Mamillius, looks over his shoulder for his parents in the same way that Mamillius will watch the disintegration of his parents' relationship in the play. The pure, compelling voice of Irene Lindh serenades the assembled with Almqvist's "The Heart's Flower," a song that sets the play's ambiguous spiritual stakes of suffering and mercy with the lines "The heart asks God why did you give this rose to me / God's heavenly answer, the blood from your heart has given the color to the rose." And then, in one of the many magnificent transitions that Bergman engineers, the bittersweet mood is reversed when the children at the party start ringing bells and calling for the play to start.

As the Shakespearean exposition begins in the foreground, the children, now wearing white-faced masks of comedy and tragedy, pull a platform bearing the host and hostess and a friend of theirs down toward the action. When the platform reaches the front of the stage, these three have become the blue-robed Leontes (the superb Börje Ahlstedt), the green-robed Polixenes (Krister Henriksson), and the charming Hermione

(Pernilla August, who played the lame servant girl in Bergman's *Fanny and Alexander* and Bergman's mother in *The Best Intentions,* and who here, draped in a vibrant-red Empire gown, radiates serenity and an irresistible generosity of spirit).

Why does Leontes, who begins the play by asking Hermione to use her charms to make his beloved brother stay at court, suddenly go berserk when she succeeds? As a tragic character, Leontes poses a theatrical problem for any director. Unlike Othello or Lear, he doesn't smolder with inner turmoil. He simply crashes and burns in a blaze of jealousy. He acts out passion's awful agitation, which Shakespeare himself records in Sonnet No. 147: "Past cure I am, now reason is past care, / And frantic mad with evermore unrest." (The sonnets were published in 1609; and *The Winter's Tale,* the thirty-fifth of Shakespeare's thirty-six plays, was first produced in 1610–11.) Bergman's Leontes suffers from the dementia of the perception of a love triangle similar to the one in which Shakespeare was caught — between the third Earl of Southampton (Henry Wriothesley), who was his patron, and the Dark Lady. Here the sexual charge of Hermione is unmistakable. Pernilla August gives Hermione a sense of ripeness and openness. She continually touches her husband's body, and he playfully drapes her red shawl around his neck; but when she turns to Polixenes the intimacy between them is also palpable. She's so comfortable with both men that if you can't understand Swedish it's not clear at first just who is husband and who is brother-in-law. The power of her connection with Polixenes hits Leontes like a brainstorm, and he suddenly begins to demonize his wife. His braying hatred is the flip side of idealized passion — the vindictive volte-face that Shakespeare makes in Sonnet No. 147:

For I have sworn thee fair, and thought thee bright,
Who art as black as hell, as dark as night.

As Leontes begins his litany of accusation, the red shawl of passion, which once connected them, now lies between them like a river of blood.

Bibi Andersson in Shakespeare's A Winter's Tale *at the Royal Dramatic Theater of Sweden in 1994, presented at the Brooklyn Academy of Music in 1995*

Leontes plots to murder his brother and settles on exiling him from his kingdom; nearly stomps his newborn daughter, Perdita, to death in her cot before sending her into uncertain exile; generates the grief that his son, Mamillius, dies from; and imprisons Hermione and then calls her before his kangaroo court, which, so it seems, kills her. Bergman handles the melodrama of this fury in brilliant collaboration with the choreographer Donya Feuer. When Leontes glimpses Hermione and Polixenes circled in a dance — a stunning image of exclusion, which evokes the furious isolation in Edvard Munch's "The Dance of Life" — a rush of stabbing anguish overcomes him; he's grabbed the live wire of possessiveness and can't let go. Leontes breaks into the circle, casting Polixenes out and embracing Hermione. He holds her at arm's length while she nestles his hand gently against her cheek. Suddenly, Leontes whispers something obscene to her, and Hermione breaks away. Leontes grabs a nearby female member of the court and begins to rape her. It's a beautifully staged and awful moment. What compounds Leontes' passion and his violence, Bergman seems to be saying, is the middle-aged king's unconscious terror of impotence. In its opening moments, the play hints at the brothers' sexual prowess when Polixenes talks to Hermione about the vigor and innocence of their idyllic youth. "You have tripp'd since," Hermione coyly jokes, and Polixenes adds, "Temptations have since then been born to 's." But Bergman makes Hermione much younger than her husband, and eliminates from the first scene any visible sign that she is nine months pregnant. Later in Act I, when Leontes overrules the Delphic oracle, which has proclaimed Hermione innocent, he flails the behemoth Sword of Justice — a gesture that broadcasts both tyranny and sexuality. Leontes' hectoring and violence are self-hypnotic gestures, magically reinforcing his sense of potency.

In his productions, Bergman always maps out a thirteen-by-twenty-foot playing area that he calls "the optical and acoustic center." Here, having cut the text to the logistical minimum and concentrated the drama on the business of living and dying, he has turned over to Feuer twice the space — twenty-six feet by forty — in which to choreograph the subtext. It's a bold collaboration, which physicalizes the multiplicity of messages and mysteries in Shakespeare's new minting of the English language. "There is movement in his text — real physical movement, which you experience in speaking it, hearing it, even working with it," Feuer says. "His language was a carrier all the time of other meanings and other messages. This is part of Shakespeare's choreographic spirit." Together, Feuer and Bergman deliver unforgettable stage pictures. When Leontes decides to put Hermione on trial, the *figuranter* (chorus members) reappear out of a bleak snowy landscape as passersby off the street: an organ-grinder, a thief, a cripple, a chimney sweep — ghostly figures whose ragged gray presence mirrors Leontes' fragmented, unreceptive self-involvement. His baby daughter's tempest-tossed journey into exile is dramatized by a billowing gray cloth hurtling around the stage, with a clipper ship held aloft on sticks, while veiled women in ribbed gray skirts writhe like waves to the sound of a wind machine as it's cranked before our eyes. In the final act Hermione is traditionally revealed to Leontes as a statue — an unreachable, idealized object, who turns into flesh and blood when she's perceived as a person, and literally comes off her pedestal. Here Hermione is carried in from the wings on a catafalque by four *figuranter,* who march at a funereal gait. The moment, like so many of Bergman's solutions, is simple and daring.

"It is a bawdy planet," Leontes says in Act I, and Bergman never lets the audience forget that in the midst of death there is life. He breaks off the gloom and apprehension of Act I with a call to dinner. The bear that has chased Antigonus as per Shakespeare's famous stage direction "Exit pursued by a bear" reappears happily for supper carrying his costume head in his hand and a little girl on his shoulder. This is, after all, a feast; and even in the last part of the play, which begins sixteen years later in a monastery with Leontes abasing himself in front of a living statue of the Virgin Mary, a laurel wreath from the Midsummer Festival is hung unobtrusively on the corner of a screen. The Madonna to whom Leontes prostrates himself is the Bleeding Maria, with a sword plunged in her heart, and her body held up in a posture of crucifixion. Bergman subtly carries the symbols of Christian rebirth through the production: the evergreen Christmas tree in the Grand Hall of Act I; the Midsummer Festival tree — a cross decorated with ivy and a Swedish flag in Act II; and, in the finale, the Crucifixion itself. In the intervening years, Leontes has tortured himself with remorse. When he rises to meet the banished Perdita, now to be married to his brother's son, Florizel, his flagellated back and stomach have bled through his shirt. Hermione, who, unbeknownst to him, has been in purdah awaiting the oracle's promise of her daughter's return, comes to life before his eyes. Leontes and Perdita fall to their knees in shock, and Leontes is held up by his brother. "Present your hand," says Paulina, who orchestrates this stage-managed resurrection. The moment is also theatrical revelation. Leontes is beyond forgiveness, and he knows it. He has accepted grief as his destiny and his due. He sits down beside Hermione and slowly, tentatively, stretches his hand over hers. Perdita does the same. "O, she's warm," Leontes says. Perdita lays her head in her mother's lap. Hermione's head brushes against Leontes' shoulder. It's an immense gesture, a miracle of the heart, which Bergman stages like a Pietà. Hermione speaks almost inaudibly to her daughter: "Where hast thou been preserv'd? where liv'd? how found / Thy father's court?" Perdita and Leontes raise Hermione up, and Perdita places her parents' hands together. They exit hand in hand to continue the conversation offstage. At that moment of salvation, snacks are announced. Life's banquet goes on.

"A sad tale's best for winter," Shakespeare says in the play. The mayhem of *The Winter's Tale,* like a horror movie's submersion in death, is meant to renew the living's sense of life. Here, in

Bergman with the set model of A Winter's Tale *at the Royal Dramatic Theater of Sweden in 1994*

the liquid Northern moonlight, Bergman calls up the spirits of Almqvist and Shakespeare and himself in one final song, the prayer "The Listening Mother of God":

> O my God, how beautiful it is,
> To hear the sound of a holy angel's voice,
> O God, how wonderful it is,
> To die to music and to song. . . .
> Quietly sink, O my holy spirit, in
> The arms of God, the Living, the Good.

On that note of grace, Time (Kristina Adolphson) rises from the front row of the orchestra section and, having opened Act II, now ends the play. She is a regal, white-haired lady in a formal black dress with a red train. She holds a cheap brass alarm clock and now sets it on the lip of the stage. As she moves upstage to leave, she looks back over her shoulder at us, and a smile plays briefly across her face. The clock's hands are at five minutes to twelve. For Shakespeare in *The Winter's Tale*, for the seventy-six-year-old Bergman, and for us in the theater, Time is almost up. In this eloquent production, imbued with the calm authority of genius, Bergman leaves us with the ticking of the clock and the urgency of forgiveness and blessing.

ACKNOWLEDGMENTS

Ingmar Bergman: An Artist's Journey was conceived in the context of the Bergman Festival held in New York City in May and June of 1995, under the patronage of their Majesties King Carl XVI Gustaf and Queen Silvia of Sweden.

The festival honored the full range of Ingmar Bergman's creative life, including his films, stage direction, writing — of both scripts and fiction — and work for television.

Absolut Vodka was the major sponsor of the Bergman Festival through its contribution to the Brooklyn Academy of Music (a not-for-profit, tax-exempt organization), which served as the festival's executive producer.

Participating organizations in the festival were:

American Museum of the Moving Image
Brooklyn Academy of Music
Film Society of Lincoln Center
The New York Public Library for
    the Performing Arts
The Museum of Modern Art
The Museum of Television & Radio
Thirteen · WNET

Additional support was provided by The Swedish Corporate Consortium: Pharmacia, Skandinaviska Enskilda Banken, Skanska, Volvo, and Scandinavian Airlines, the official airline; New York State Council for the Humanities; The American-Scandinavian Foundation; and The Bernard Osher Foundation. Swedish government support was provided by The Swedish Ministry of Culture; The Swedish Film Institute; The Swedish Institute; The Swedish Ministry for Foreign Affairs; and The Swedish Information Service.

The honorary chair of the Bergman Festival was Dag Sebastian Ahlander, Consul General of Sweden. Festival chairs were: Michael J. Fuchs, Chairman and CEO, Home Box Office, and Christina Ofverholm-Molitéus.

Photo Credits

Bengt Wanselius, pages x, 17, 19, 89, 90, 92, 95, 107, 108, 110, 143, 147, 151, 152, 156, 157, 159; The Royal Dramatic Theater of Sweden, pages 21, 138, 140; Svensk Filmindustri, pages 4, 15, 40, 47, 50, 55, 58, 65, 67, 102; Arne Carlsson, pages 113, 119, 123. The photographs on pages 6, 9, 26, 28–29, 33, 35, 38, 60, 63, 70, 71, 72–73, 75, 81, 82–83, 85, 100, 115, 117, 122, 127, 130, 133 are taken from *Images: My Life in Film*, by Ingmar Bergman, New York: Arcade Publishing, 1994.